Scripture and
Social Action

Used by permission of Bill Sanders of THE KANSAS CITY STAR

Scripture and Social Action

Bruce D. Rahtjen

ABINGDON PRESS
Nashville   New York

SCRIPTURE AND SOCIAL ACTION

Copyright © 1966 by Abingdon Press

Library of Congress Catalog Card Number: 66-20458

Scripture quotations unless otherwise noted are from the Revised
Standard Version of the Bible, copyrighted 1946 and 1952 by the
Division of Christian Education, National Council of Churches,
and are used by permission.

SET UP, PRINTED, AND BOUND BY THE
PARTHENON PRESS, AT NASHVILLE,
TENNESSEE, UNITED STATES OF AMERICA

To my mother

Anne Miller Rahtjen

Preface

What does Scripture have to do with social action? More than you might think at first glance. A church that tries to have one without the other is in real trouble! Social reform divorced from biblical faith is a shallow humanism. Belief in the Bible which does not shine forth in social concern is a pious fraud.

This is not to say that the translation of biblical ideas into social reforms is an easy or painless process. Quite the contrary! The task is as difficult as it is unavoidable. Consequently there are already several books available on the subject.

Some of the books take one social problem, such as race relations or Communism, and draw out all the biblical material which can be applied to it. Others concentrate on the social implications of one part of the Bible, such as the Sermon on the Mount or the prophecy of Amos. Still others use the Bible as the springboard for a detailed study of Christian ethics.

This book does none of these things. It simply raises three questions for discussion: 1. What are the problems involved in applying biblical material several thousand years old to problems as new as this morning's headlines? 2. How did the church come to its present understanding of the meaning of the Bible, its own role as a social witness, and the relationship of the one to the other? 3. What are the biblical doctrines which lead us into social action, and what do they require of us today?

The purpose of the book is not to provide neat answers for these questions but to clarify the issues and set the reader to the task of finding his own answers. Resources for this task will be found in the notes and the selected bibliography. For those who wish to use the book as a study guide, discussion questions have been suggested for each chapter.

Many people have helped in the preparation of this manuscript. The project was undertaken largely through the encouragement of Dr. Cecil Culver and the Rev. Wallace Shook. I am grateful to my colleagues, John M. Swomley, Jr., E. Dale Dunlap, and W. Paul Jones, for their helpful criticism of the text. Finally, I am grateful to the Saint Paul School of Theology Methodist for allowing me the time to write the book, and to Mrs. Arlene Barber, Mrs. Julie Goldman, and Mrs. Beverley Goldsworthy for their excellent secretarial help.

BRUCE D. RAHTJEN

Contents

1 The Dilemma of the Old Testament 11

2 Amos or Ezra? 18

3 Christ Is the Yardstick 38

4 Deists, Calvinists, and Wesley 52

5 Social Action—and Reaction 62

6 The Gospel for Today 79

7 The Whole Gospel for the Whole Man 93

8 Where Do We Begin? 108

Notes 125

Questions for Discussion 133

Selected Bibliography 137

Index 143

1

The Dilemma of the Old Testament

Most Christians find the Old Testament the most difficult part of the Bible to understand. Certainly, there are difficult passages in portions of the New Testament. The book of Revelation by itself is enough to test the perseverance of a saint. But the Old Testament as a whole poses such numerous and difficult problems, that many people just give up in dismay when they first attempt to read it.

The Old Testament is important to us for a number of reasons. In the first place, it provides a theological background for the New Testament. The doctrine of God, and certain basic elements of the doctrine of man found in the New Testament, come directly from the Old Testament. Furthermore there is a very close historical link between the two Testaments. The Old Testament was the Bible of Jesus. Most of the members of the early church were Jews. Several of the New Testament writers made extensive use of a Greek translation of the Old Testament in their work.[1]

Since the Old Testament held such an important

place historically and theologically in the early church, it was soon declared to be a part of the Christian Bible. It was accepted on the same basis as the Gospels and the writings of Paul as being the Word of God. It is still considered as such today. Yet we find that it contains a great deal of material which is unacceptable in terms of our Christian faith.

Christians must be very careful in using Old Testament material as a basis for preaching, or as a basis for a standard of morality. On the one hand we find in the Old Testament the Ten Commandments as a basis of personal and national morality. On the other hand we see great delight at the clever treachery of Samson (Judg. 16) and Jael (Judg. 4), and the slaughter of Israel's enemies which resulted therefrom. On the one hand we see several prophets talking about the time when lions and lambs shall lie down together, when men shall beat their swords into plow shares and their spears into pruning hooks. On the other hand the book of Esther recounts with great gusto and relish the slaughter of thousands upon thousands of Israel's enemies by Jews under the leadership of Mordecai. On one hand we find the people of Israel being urged to deal kindly and gently with the strangers and sojourners in their midst. On the other hand we find Ezra preaching against the marriage of Jews to foreign wives and insisting that such foreign wives and their children be sent back to their homelands immediately.

It is not necessary to jump from one part of the

Old Testament to another to find a contrast between perfectly acceptable (and even laudable) principles, and sentiments which amaze and dismay the modern Christian reader. For example, Ps. 137 is often used in Christian churches because of the beauty of its language and the touching sentiments of the Jews who are longing for their homeland, and who proclaim their intense loyalty to Jerusalem. On the other hand no Christian congregation today can bring itself to use the entire psalm in worship, for the last three verses of it take quite a different tone from the first six. After a denunciation of several of the enemies of Israel it is suggested that the brains of enemy children should be dashed out on the rocks!

Any attempt on the part of a Christian to use the Old Testament must involve a great deal of careful selection. We feel that the Old Testament is the Word of God, and that we are therefore bound by its commandments. And yet, there are many of the commandments of the Old Testament which we do not take seriously at all today. To illustrate our point let us look at Lev. 19. In this single chapter there are nearly two dozen commandments of one sort or another. Some of them, we would insist, are commandments which are binding on all of us. For example, we are told to honor our fathers and mothers. We are urged to avoid idolatry. We are warned not to steal, to deal falsely with others, nor to lie to one another. We are not to oppress or rob our neighbors, nor to tip the scales of justice in favor of the rich or the powerful. We are to avoid slandering our neighbors and bearing grudges. All of us would agree that these are rules and regulations which should govern our lives. However, in the same chapter we find a number of commandments which we feel have no authority for us today at all. We are told, for example, that the fruit of every tree shall be forbidden to its owner for the first four years that it bears. Only in the fifth year is the fruit to be eaten by the owner. The eating of meat with blood in it is prohibited. Verse 27 prohibits the trimming of beards and the cutting of the hair at the temples.

No Christian today feels that this latter group of commandments is binding upon him in any way. When we order a rare steak in a restaurant and have it served with blood standing on the platter, we have no feeling of having violated one of the laws of God. The man who sinks his teeth into a luscious apple from a tree which he has pruned and fertilized for years, and which has just borne its first fruit, does not feel that he is taking anything away from God in enjoying the apple. The Christian who sees an Orthodox Jewish rabbi with a full beard and the hair at his temples hanging down to his shoulders in two long curls feels that this man is somehow out of touch with reality in today's world, and that he is taking too literally a passage which no longer has any immediate relevance.

On what basis do we decide that the commandment not to shave is less important and less commanding than the commandment to love our neighbors as ourselves? They are presented in the same chapter of the same book with the same force. It does not answer the question to say that the first law is irrelevant in terms of our modern world and therefore can be disregarded today, whereas the second is still timely. If we determine what laws are relevant by examining what men do today, we should have to say that "love your neighbor as yourself" is as irrelevant as anything in the Old Testament! Yet we feel that this law has some moral claim on us, whereas many other Old Testament rules and regulations do not. Do we really have a basis for choosing what to obey and what to ignore, or do we simply read the Old Testament "cafeteria style," choosing what appeals to us and discarding the rest?

What sort of guidelines are appropriate? Do we accept the picture of God as the author of warfare and slaughter, which we find in Joshua and Judges, or do we believe with Hosea, that the most important characteristic of God is his love? As Christians we take it for granted that there are certain passages which are more significant than others. For example, the description of the Suffering Servant in Isa. 53 is of great importance in terms of Christian theology. In it we see the meaning of the death of Christ. It is often used as a scripture lesson during Lent, especially on Good Friday. But our estimate of this chapter's importance is not shared by Jewish theologians. They commonly refer to it as an interesting "dead end" in Hebrew theology, which never was carried any further.[2] On the other hand the story of the Exodus, which is only of secondary importance to us, is the very basis of one of the most important Jewish celebrations, the Passover.[3]

It is obvious that we must have some yardstick against which to measure the material in the Old Testament. The "cafeteria" method of choosing what to follow and what to reject leaves too much to chance and puts too much faith in our fragile human nature. When we are asked to choose between loving our neighbors or giving up rare steak, it is obvious which has a claim on us. But our choices are not always that easy. Where do we look when we want some guidance on the issue of race? Do we choose a statement of the love of God for all people (see Amos 9:7 and Isa. 49:6), or do we choose the warning in Lev. 19 to keep separate the different breeds of cattle, and even different varieties of seeds, and different clothing fibers? In a problem of this sort our final decisions are by no means clear.

The first principle on which we must base our selection of Old Testament material is that of depth-analysis of the material in question. We should not begin to weigh the value of any passage until we have used all available resources of scholarship to shed light on its original meaning.

Secondly, after we have determined the true meaning of the passage in terms of its original context,

16

we must evaluate that meaning in terms of our Christian faith. That is to say, we must read the Old Testament christologically. And whether or not a particular rule or regulation is binding upon us depends on its relationship to God's act in Christ. In the next two chapters we shall try to discover just what these two principles mean.

2

Amos or Ezra?

As you unroll the morning newspaper, a headline in large type catches your attention. A well-known national political leader has just made an important speech. You read through the paragraphs of the article to find out what the man had to say. When you finish, you make a judgment concerning the validity of his comments.

Before making up your mind concerning the speech, you have to ask yourself a number of questions. Who is the man who made the speech? What is his political party? How does the content of his speech relate to the principles of that party? What is the relationship of the speech to other recent and forthcoming political events? Is the man running for office? If so, is this an attempt to convince people to vote for him? To whom was the speech made? Was an attempt made to tailor the content of the speech to the immediate audience? What is the relationship of this speech to other things said by the same man, on the same general topic, during his political career? Only when you know the answers to these questions can you evaluate the true meaning of the speech.

Let me illustrate with one concrete example. Early in 1964 the national press carried quotations from two leading political figures, both of whom said, "Government-spending should be reduced!" On the surface it would seem that these men agreed on what should be done with the national budget. But in order to evaluate these two statements, you have to know who the two men were. One was Lyndon Johnson, who was working to get approval for his budget from the conservative southern Democrats in Congress. The other was Barry Goldwater, who was in the midst of his drive for the 1964 Republican presidential nomination. Both men said the same thing, but what they actually meant was quite different! A twenty-first-century historian, analyzing the statements, would have to know a great deal about the men who made them and the conditions under which they were made, before he could assess them properly.

Obviously there is a great deal of difference between a political speech and the Old Testament. But in one important respect they are alike. Before we can understand the meaning of any passage in the Old Testament, there are a number of things that we must know about it. Who is the author? When did he write? What was the religious and political situation in Israel at the time? Where was the passage written? To what audience was it originally addressed? What was the occasion which called forth this particular piece of literature? What is its relationship to the rest of the work of this author and to the rest of the Old Testament?

Only when we have the answers to these questions can we understand what the particular passage meant to the people who first heard or read it. When we find out what the passage meant in its original context, then we are able to apply it to our situation today by means of analogy.

When we go to the Old Testament for guidance concerning a problem which faces us today, we must use the process described above in evaluating the various levels of material which we find. For example, we may want to find out what the Old Testament has to say concerning the rights and wrongs of integration and segregation. Both an integrationist and a segregationist can go to the Old Testament and find there material which will appear to back up their points of view. Since both points of view can be "strengthened" on the basis of Old Testament material, must we give up the Old Testament as a source for any biblical witness concerning the solution to our problems? No! We can still receive help from the Old Testament if we are willing to analyze its material in the right way. We must take all the material which we can find on both sides of the issue and see how it fits into the overall pattern of Old Testament theology. On the basis of the meanings of the passages in their original contexts, we may be able to discover what they mean for us today. Let's take a look at the history behind the passages most often quoted by integrationists and segregationists.

There are passages throughout the Old Testament which seem to give support to a divinely ordained separation of the races of mankind. In the book of Genesis there are references to curses which were placed upon certain men. The implication of these passages is that their descendants, because of the curse which was upon them, were to be an inferior group of people.[4] Therefore they would not be entitled to all the rights and privileges of other people. The remainder of the Pentateuch indicates, in a number of places, that the Hebrews were not to associate closely with the people who lived around them, nor to enter into marriages with the daughters of those people.[5] Some of the prophets denounced foreign nations passionately and declared that God had destined them only for destruction.[6] In the books of Ezra and Nehemiah we find a number of statements in which foreigners are denounced. The preaching of Ezra deals specifically with Hebrew men who have married women from foreign countries. These marriages are denounced, and Ezra insists that the women who have married Hebrew men must be sent home along with their children.[7] In order to discover the validity of these passages for us today, we must examine the history of the Hebrew people in terms of their relationship with the nations around them.

When the Hebrews first settled in the land of

Canaan, they were not able to take the entire country at one time. They settled the areas which they were able to occupy with a minimum of bloodshed and left the large cities alone.[8] One by one, the large cities of Canaan began to fall into the hands of the Hebrews. But the process of taking the cities was a long and drawn-out one. The last city to fall to the Hebrews was Jerusalem, which was captured by David, nearly three hundred years after the Hebrews first entered Canaan.[9]

This meant that the Hebrews were living in a land where they were surrounded by Canaanites on all sides. Naturally, as time went on, they began to have cultural relationships with the Canaanites. Before long there were other neighbors who also crowded in upon them. Among these were the Philistines and the Phoenicians. The language and culture of the Hebrews were very much like those of the people around them.[10] The only thing which distinguished the Hebrews from their neighbors was their religion. For this reason it was necessary for the Hebrews to keep to themselves in order to keep their religion pure. The religious leaders of the nation could not allow the pagan practices of the neighboring peoples to become a part of the worship of God.

Therefore the Hebrews were told not to mingle with their neighbors. A great many of the rules and regulations in the Old Testament owe their origin to this fact. For example, the Hebrews were forbidden to eat the flesh of the pig. The reason for this was that the pig was the sacred animal of the Canaanites. Often, when a Canaanite altar is found, there are pig bones nearby. Similarly, the Hebrews were forbidden to eat shellfish or any of the salt water food fish which did not have scales. These foods were the main supply of protein for the Phoenicians and the Philistines.

Because of the emphasis on religious purity, the Hebrews were quite conscious of the difference between themselves and other nations. For a long time they had the feeling that God was concerned only with them. He had brought them out of the land of Egypt and established them in Canaan because they were his people. They felt that because he had chosen them, he had rejected all other nations.

By the beginning of the era of the great prophets, this idea had begun to change somewhat. In the preaching of Amos, who began his ministry in 750 B.C., we find a passage which says that God cares as much about other nations as he does about Israel.[11] The people of Israel, he says, are no different in the eyes of the Lord than the Ethiopians. Furthermore, there is no reason for the Hebrews to boast of the fact that the Lord brought them out of Egypt and into the land of Canaan. Amos reminds his people that the Lord also brought the Philistines from their homeland and the Syrians (Arameans) from theirs.[12] In the book of Isaiah we find several other references to God's concern for foreign nations. Chapter 2:2-3

23

says that Jerusalem will become the center of worship for all nations. All the peoples of the world will say, "Come, let us go up the mountain of the Lord, to the house of the God of Jacob; that he may teach us his ways and that we may walk in his paths." The author then goes on to describe God as the judge of all nations who will decide their disputes and settle their differences, so that there will be no more warfare, and "nation shall not lift up sword against nation, neither shall they learn war any more." A similar passage is found in Isa. 25:6, where the mountain of the Lord, i.e., Mount Zion in Jerusalem, will be a place of feasting for all nations. There is a brief reference in Isa. 18:7 to foreign peoples who will bring sacrifices to God in Jerusalem. A century later the prophet Jeremiah (12:14-17) referred to God's concern for the neighbors of Israel. The prophets said that if these people would repent of their paganism and worship God, they would be accepted by him and he would love them as his own.

But during the ministry of Jeremiah the entire theological position of the Hebrews was drastically reshaped by history. For several generations the Hebrew nations of Israel and Judah had been living under the sword of the great powers of Mesopotamia. When Amos preached to the northern kingdom of Israel, he warned the people that the Assyrians were a serious threat to their existence. He told them that if they did not change their ways, God would use the Assyrians as his means of punishing them for idolatry

24

and paganism.[13] The people laughed at Amos, because they knew that God would protect them no matter what happened.

But in 721, just twenty-nine years after Amos began his ministry, the Assyrians captured Israel and slaughtered many of the people. Those who remained were deported and scattered all over the Assyrian empire. From all sections of the far-flung Assyrian empire people were brought in to take the place of those who had been deported. The idea behind this move was quite simple. The Assyrians felt that if people had no national or cultural identity they would not cooperate in planning a revolution against the Assyrian power. And an empire which extended over thousands of miles always had the problem of keeping the provinces in the outlying areas in line. Nothing was left of what had once been the ten northern tribes and is later referred to as "the ten lost tribes of Israel." The people who remained after the Assyrian purge were a mixed group culturally, nationally, religiously, and linguistically. The only thing they had in common was the place where they lived. Therefore they became known as Samaritans, named for Samaria, the capital city of the province. Because they were a very mixed group, they were disliked and avoided by the Judeans who wanted to preserve the religious and cultural heritage of their ancestors. These were the seeds out of which grew the bitter hatred between Jews and Samaritans, which we know so well from the New Testament.

In 586, the city of Jerusalem fell, just as Israel had fallen in 721. But in the meanwhile there had been a change of leadership in Mesopotamia. For in 612, the great empire of Assyria was destroyed. Its place was taken by the Babylonians under the leadership of Nebuchadnezzar. This change was very important as far as the history of the Hebrews was concerned. For the Babylonians did not share the ideas of the Assyrians as to how an outlying province should be kept free from revolutions. The plan of the Babylonians was to leave most of the people just where they were and to let them live in peace. But the leaders of the nations were potentially dangerous to the peace of the empire. Therefore a small percentage of the people of each province was exiled and taken to Babylon. Although they were a small part of the whole population, they represented the leaders in every area of life. They were installed in very comfortable quarters in the city of Babylon and allowed to live their own lives there, just as they wished.[14] The only things that they could not do were to return to their native lands or to correspond with people there who might be trying to start a revolution against the imperial government.

The Babylonian exile of the Hebrew leaders meant that all the important priests and other religious leaders were living in Babylon for the better part of a century. They were not able to return to their homeland, but they were able to preserve, in Babylon, the religion of their ancestors. Therefore, when

26

the period of exile was over, the religion of Judah had not died or been drastically changed. But the fact that the city of Jerusalem had fallen and the temple had been destroyed by foreigners, made a great deal of difference in the religious outlook of the people who carried on the traditions of Judah in Babylon.

One of the characteristics of the religion of the Jewish leaders during the exile was an intensified interest in ritual. Previously none of the ritual of the temple had ever been written down. It had circulated in oral tradition and was handed down from father to son without ever being committed to writing. Every Judean priest had learned the ritual and the fine points of worship by serving as an apprentice in the temple under the supervision of his father. For the only way to enter the priesthood was to be born into the family of a priest. Now it was no longer possible to teach the laws of ritual and temple worship to young men in the temple itself, for the temple was destroyed, and the priests were many hundreds of miles away from home. In order to make sure that the ritual was neither forgotten nor changed, the priests spent a great deal of their time in exile writing down all the priestly rules and regulations. In doing so they drew on oral traditions which had been circulating for a considerable period of time.

These priestly leaders had the idea that the reason for the fall of Jerusalem was that God was displeased with the way in which the sacrifices had been offered.

27

Perhaps, if they had been able to make a sacrificial offering for every sin that had been committed, God would not have become angry with them and allowed a foreign nation to destroy them. Perhaps they had been careless in the precise ritual which they had used in making sacrifices, and this had made God angry with them. It was necessary, therefore, to have all the priestly instructions written out as completely as possible. In this way, if they should have an opportunity to rebuild the temple in the future, all the proper sacrifices could be made. Then God would never again become angry with his people and allow a foreign army to destroy the temple.

This intense interest in priestly ritual and tradition on the part of all the religious leaders in exile left no room for consideration of God's concern for persons. The words of Amos, for example, were largely forgotten or ignored. Amos had said that one of the reasons that God would punish his people was because of the injustice in society, where the poor people were being trodden underfoot by the rich. Furthermore he said that God would not allow mistreatment of one nation by a bloodthirsty foreign power. In his opening temple address in Bethel he said that God was planning to punish several of the nations surrounding Israel, because they had hated their enemies and had slaughtered some of them.[15] But the intense preoccupation of the religious leaders with liturgy and the fine points of sacrifice left no room for any consideration of God's love for men.

The priests had no interest at all in the relationship of God to any nation except Judah.

At the same time, all the exiled leaders of Judah shared an intense dislike for the Babylonians because of what had taken place. And this hatred and distrust of Babylonians very quickly spread to all other nations as well. The Jewish theologians thought that somehow or other the Babylonians had managed to pervert the will of God by destroying his temple. Therefore it was natural that God would hate the Babylonians and wish to have them destroyed as quickly as possible. All the religious concerns of the Jewish priests began to turn inward. The only important religious fact as far as they were concerned was the covenant between their nation and God. Certainly, while they were in Babylon, God did not want them to mix with the pagans who worshiped there. If the nation of Judah should be reestablished in the future, God would want it to remain pure and undefiled by any pagan influences. It was necessary for them to keep to themselves and to hate foreigners, because God had chosen them alone of all the peoples of the world. Therefore we find them preserving in their writings—a goodly part of the book of Genesis —traditions that God had cursed certain groups of people from the beginning and had made them inferior to his chosen people, the Jews.[16]

But once again, history was used by God to bring about a change in the situation of his people. About 540 B.C., the nation of Babylon fell before the attacks

29

of the Medes and Persians. Soon the ruler of Babylon was the Persian king, Cyrus. Cyrus did not share the opinions of either the Assyrians or the Babylonians concerning the prevention of revolutions in outlying provinces.

It was the policy of Cyrus to send home from Babylon all the descendants of the exiled leaders from the various provinces. He allowed the people of each province to rebuild their cities and to reconstruct their centers of worship. The priests of each nation were allowed to reestablish whatever services of worship they wished. Cyrus placed upon the throne of each province the man who had the best hereditary claim to the royal line. However, he instituted a system of checks and balances to limit the power of each hereditary ruler, known as the satrap, so that a revolution would not be forthcoming.

When the leaders of the Jews returned from exile and rebuilt the city of Jerusalem and their temple, there was some change in the theological outlook of the nation. The interest in liturgy was very strong, but it no longer crowded out all other considerations. A number of the religious leaders in Israel began to see the plan of God as involving far more than the destiny of one small nation. Just before the exile the prophet Habakkuk commented on the way in which God was using the major world powers to accomplish his will among the Hebrews. Just below the surface in Habakkuk's writings lies the question, "Does God have a far wider and more important purpose for his people than appears at first glance?" [17]

When the Jews returned from exile, the leading prophet of that period, the Second Isaiah, gave an affirmative answer to Habakkuk's question.[18] This prophet saw the plan of God as a worldwide scheme of salvation. He insisted that God dealt lovingly with all nations and was concerned about the destiny of all men. He referred to King Cyrus as "the anointed one of God" who had been divinely appointed to capture the city of Babylon and send the Jews back to their homeland.[19]

In Isa. 49, the prophet outlines his understanding of God's plan in detail. God had established his relationship with Judah and had brought his people through their many trials, including a recent period of purification in exile, in order to use them as a means of salvation for the entire world.

And now the Lord says, who formed me from the womb to be his servant, to bring Jacob back to him, and that Israel might be gathered to him, for I am honored in the eyes of the Lord, and my God has become my strength—he says: "It is too light a thing that you should be my servant to raise up the tribes of Jacob and to restore the preserved of Israel; I will give you as a light to the nations, that my salvation may reach to the end of the earth." [20]

In Isa. 53, the prophet refers to Israel as the Suffering Servant of God, who will suffer before all the nations of the earth, that all men might see what God

31

is doing with his servant and turn unto him in repentance and faithfulness.

This was a far cry from the narrow nationalism of the priestly writers of the exile. Now God's relationship with Israel was seen as a means to an end. The fact that he had dealt directly with Israel was only a reflection of his concern for all mankind. It appears that this idea was well received and widely accepted during the time of the Second Isaiah and immediately afterward.

But this was a temporary situation. Sometime in the middle of the fifth century B.C. there was a sudden change in the attitude of the Jews toward other people. The intense nationalism which had marked the priestly writing of the exile returned as the dominant theme of the late fifth century. The books of Ezra and Nehemiah are filled with intense bitterness against all foreigners. At the time of Ezra there was a campaign to prevent the intermarriage of Jews with foreign women and to terminate such marriages which had already taken place. All foreign wives and their children would be sent back immediately to the land from which the women had come.

Why the change? Why did the universalism of the Second Isaiah give way to the intense and narrow nationalism of Ezra and Nehemiah? We are not *sure* what the reasons were, but some scholars have offered an educated guess. It appears that the Jerusalem temple may have been destroyed a second time in 486

B.C., just one hundred years after the original destruction and exile. The Bible makes no direct reference to any such destruction. On the other hand, if we try to compare the chronology of Ezra and Nehemiah with the chronology of Haggai and Zechariah, we run into an impossible situation. There is no way that the historical material in these four books can be reconciled. It appears that there is a whole period of Old Testament history which has been deliberately chopped out of the biblical accounts by someone who did not want future generations to know what had happened. We do have some outside evidence that the Persian rulers of the early fifth century did not share Cyrus' enthusiasm for the worship of various gods by the people of the provinces in their own temples. The Emperor Xerxes notes, in his records of the first year of his reign (486-85), that he went to Palestine and Egypt from Persia, destroying many temples of gods other than his own as he went.[21] It may very well be that the temple of the Jews in Jerusalem was at least partially destroyed by Xerxes. This would explain the intense bitterness which suddenly arose against people from all other nations. It would explain why the Jewish theologians turned away from the Second Isaiah and his notion that God is very much concerned with the welfare of *all* peoples and *all* nations.

Whatever the reason for the change, we know that Ezra and Nehemiah and their followers had no use for foreigners. And throughout the books of Ezra and Nehemiah we find many references to the wisdom of keeping the Jews separate from all other people.

Interestingly enough, there were those who stood up against Ezra and Nehemiah and insisted that God *did* care for *all* men. One man in this tradition was the writer who took the ancient story of the prophet Jonah and used it as a piece of propaganda for "universalism."

He told the story of God's commission to Jonah to go to Nineveh, the capital of Assyria and the wickedest city in the world, to ask the people to repent. Jonah did not want to go, because he felt that the people of Nineveh, being foreigners, were beneath contempt. But God would not take no for an answer, and Jonah was forced to do his bidding. When Jonah arrived in the city of Nineveh, he did as God had told him and warned the people that they should repent. But all that he did was to tell them *once* that God had demanded their repentance, and that they would be punished if they failed to comply. Then, confident of the failure of his mission, he sat down outside the city to enjoy the sight of the destruction.

Jonah waited for some time to see the destruction which God would visit upon this wicked city. Surely, the punishment of such an evil place would be spectacular! But to his utter amazement the people repented of their sins and turned to God. Not only did they don sackcloth and ashes as symbols of their repentance, but they even put sackcloth and ashes on their animals. Because of their repentance, there was no destruction. Jonah was furious that he had been denied the treat of watching the city's destruction. In disgust he sat outside the city walls and sulked.

As Jonah sulked, God looked upon him and decided to teach him a lesson. As he sat there in the hot sunshine, a plant began to grow next to him at a very rapid rate. At the end of one day the plant was so large that it shaded Jonah from the sun. The next day it was attacked by a worm, who destroyed it completely. Jonah was unhappy that the plant was no longer there. Then the Lord appeared to Jonah and asked him if he missed the plant. Jonah replied that he did. The Lord then asked Jonah to consider the meaning of what had happened. If Jonah was able to miss a plant, which had been there for only one day, and was sorry that it had been destroyed, how would he expect God to feel if he had to destroy an entire city of people whom he had created and whom he loved? The application of this story to the attitudes of Ezra and Nehemiah is obvious.

Another story from the same period, which makes the same point, is the book of Ruth. Ruth was a widow from Moab who came to Israel because of her faithfulness to her Hebrew mother-in-law and then married a Hebrew man. The grandson of Ruth and her Hebrew husband was Jesse, the father of King David. Now the Hebrews who wanted to boast of the purity of their ancestry in the time of Ezra an-

35

nounced that they could trace their ancestry all the way back to King David. There was no greater claim to purity of ancestry than this. But the author of the book of Ruth pointed out slyly that David himself had a Moabite great-grandmother. If David himself was the indirect result of a union between a woman from Moab and a man from Judah, how could the marriage of a Jewish man and a woman from Moab be wrong, in the time of Ezra?

In spite of these isolated attempts to prove that God did love all mankind, the opinions of Ezra won the day. Jewish nationalism did not decline after Ezra's time.

When we examine the history of the theological doctrines of nationalism and universalism in the Old Testament, we see that nationalism and the insistence on "racial purity" came at periods when the Hebrews were in violent reaction against specific mistreatment at the hands of foreigners. During the rest of Hebrew history, the Hebrews affirmed God's love and concern for all mankind. Some of their leading theologians, e.g., Amos and the authors of Ruth and Jonah, held this position even in the times of greatest stress and danger. Even the harsh nationalism of Ezra was unable to suppress completely belief in God's universal love for man. Therefore, from the historical point of view, we find ourselves inclined toward the position of Amos rather than that of Ezra.

But we also have a distinct feeling that Old Testament universalism is theologically more acceptable than the narrow, hate-filled preaching of Ezra. And here we are introducing a new dimension into the discussion. We are able to sort out the relationship among the various theological ideas discussed in terms of a thorough understanding of the history and development of Old Testament theology. When we come to make a value judgment about the relative merits of two theological ideas, we imply a yardstick by which doctrines can be measured and one can be declared superior to another. This yardstick must be applied, after we have used all the tools of scholarship to illuminate the passages in question. We have now come to the point where we must discuss the nature of the theological yardstick which the Christian uses in evaluating Old Testament material.

3

Christ Is the Yardstick

For the Christian all theology is Christology. That is to say, the way we know God is through Jesus Christ. To say this does not deny that it is possible for God to reveal himself through nature or through direct revelation to man. Our trinitarian confessions of faith affirm our belief that we know God as Father, i.e., as Creator, and as Holy Spirit, i.e., through direct encounter. But the statement that we know God as Son means that we *recognize* the revelations of God in his creation or in personal encounter, because we have *first* known him through his revelation in Jesus Christ. This means that the revelation of God in Christ is our norm for natural and personal revelations.

Let us examine some possible ways of understanding the revelation of God through nature. A small child is very ill with a mysterious disease. The doctors have used all their skill and knowledge in vain. No treatment seems to do any good. Just as the doctors are about to give up hope, the child begins to rally. Little by little, strength returns to the fevered and diseased body. Eventually the child recovers entirely from the disease. None of the doctors is able to give an adequate explanation for what has happened. The child's parents, being devout church members, are firmly convinced that it is the power of God which has healed their child from the disease.

Our second example is that of a violent earthquake. In the course of the earthquake the greatest part of a large city is destroyed. Hundreds of people lose their lives, and thousands more are injured. An evangelist who has been preaching in a storefront gospel tabernacle says that he could have predicted something like this a long time ago. Because of the wickedness of this city, God has chosen to destroy it. The reason for the earthquake, he states, is the drinking, dancing, and gambling which have been going on in the city, in spite of his preaching.

For our third example we move to a Pacific island inhabited by a tribe of rather primitive people. On the island is a volcano which has been inactive for many years. Suddenly the volcano erupts. The village at the foot of the mountain is destroyed, and many of the people are killed. The religious leader of the tribe announces that the god who lives in the volcano has become angry because the people have ignored him. Therefore, he says, it is necessary to make a human sacrifice in order to pacify the angry deity.

In each one of these examples we have a phenomenon of nature and a theological explanation of it. In each case the natural phenomenon is seen as an act of God. From our Christian frame of reference, we should say that the explanation concerning the recovery of the child is probably valid. We would have some grave doubts about the validity of the explanation of the earthquake. We would certainly say that the explanation of the volcanic eruption is totally false. The basis on which we make this judgment is our knowledge of God through Jesus Christ. When we measure the phenomenon and the explanation in terms of our understanding of God as he is revealed in Christ, we are able to say "yes" or "no" in terms of Christology.

In the same way we judge *personal* revelations on the basis of a christological norm. On the one hand we have a young man who feels that he has been called to enter the Christian ministry. He has been avoiding the ministry as a vocation and has been preparing for medicine or for engineering. But somehow or other he feels that the call of God is so strong that he cannot ignore it, and he changes his direction to prepare for service in the church. On the other hand we see the same young man standing on an observation deck on top of a very high building. As he looks down into the streets of the city below, he feels a sudden urge to jump. He fights off this feeling and grips the handrail more tightly. In a moment the feeling is gone, and he wonders why he had it. In assessing these two thoughts which have preoccupied him, our young friend says that his call to the ministry is a direct revelation from God. On the other hand he defines his urge to jump from a tall

40

building as a psychological quirk which has no particular significance. On what basis does he say that his compulsion to enter the ministry is a revelation from God and his compulsion to jump from a high building is not? The answer is that he judges each of these urges or compulsions in terms of God's revelation in Christ.

As Christ is our yardstick for evaluating the revelation of God in nature and in personal experience, so he is also the yardstick for our interpretation of the Old Testament. As Christians we must read the Old Testament christologically.

But in saying that we must have a christological view of the Old Testament we must be very careful to define our terms. For a great deal of violence has been done to the meaning of the Old Testament under the banner of "christological interpretation." There is one rather "far-out" branch of Protestantism which sees no use for the Old Testament at all, except to point precisely to the person and mission of Jesus Christ. I have seen an Old Testament church school course for high school students which does absolutely nothing but point out the appearances of Jesus in every one of the books of the Old Testament. For some books this becomes very difficult indeed. The Book of Esther, for example, does not even contain a direct reference to God himself! But the writers in this curriculum suggest that Mordecai is not really Mordecai at all, but a very thinly disguised Jesus Christ.[22] According to this point of view the

41

prophet Isaiah was not really speaking to the people of his own time at all. He had nothing to say to those who were listening to his preaching at the time. His only function was to tell people of a future generation about the coming of Christ. Similarly, the stories in the historical section of the Old Testament cannot be read at face value. For example, the only reason that Moses lifted up a golden serpent on a stick in the wilderness was to represent the crucifixion of our Lord.

This kind of Old Testament interpretation, which ignores the meaning of the passage in its context and substitutes a christological allegory for it, is entirely indefensible.[23] We must allow the Old Testament to say what it says. We must understand each passage in terms of the context in which it is set and the circumstances which brought it forth. When we have understood the context of a passage, we must be faithful to that context in interpreting it. But in doing so, we must evaluate the meaning of each passage for today in terms of a christological view of history. Another way of saying the same thing is that we must view history from the point of view of a Christian *typology*.

What on earth is a "typology"? Actually it is nothing but a sophisticated seventy-five–cent word for a very simple and understandable interpretation of history. History is the listing of events of the past. But the writer of history must choose which events to include and which to ignore, on the basis of an

42

understanding of what history is all about. If he is going to be an interpretive historian, he must point out the relationship which one event has to another. But one event in history has a relationship to another event only insofar as both of them are related to an overall *meaning* of history. Individual events have no real meaning nor any relationship to one another, unless the historian sees them in terms of *one* event which gives meaning to all of history. This event, which might be called the *crucial* event in history, can be defined in the following way: 1. It is the most important event which has taken place in history. 2. It is the event which gives history its meaning. 3. It divides all other history into "before" and "after." 4. Events which have taken place before this crucial event are seen as important because of the way in which they lead up to *the* event. 5. Events which have taken place after *the* event are important because they point back to *the* event and show its importance.

The events which come before the crucial event of history are referred to as proto*types* of it, and events which take place afterward are referred to as post-*types*. Hence the term "typology."

Let's see how this idea of typology in history works out in terms of American history. What would be the crucial event of American history? Obviously it would have to be the revolution of 1776 and the founding of the American Republic at that time.

Any event coming before 1776 which seemed to be

43

a preparation for the American Revolution, would therefore be interpreted as a prototype of it. For example, there is the story of the Charter Oak of Hartford, Connecticut, coming from 1687. In that year the governor of Connecticut, Edmund Androus, demanded, on the authority of King James II, that the charter of Connecticut be returned. Turning the charter over to him would mean the removal of the guarantees of freedom which had been given to the colonists. Therefore the people of the colony refused to hand over the charter. It was taken from the authorities and hidden in a hollow oak tree in the city of Hartford. Since it could not be found, the freedoms it guaranteed were not revoked. This event is a prototype of the revolution, because it shows exactly the same kind of spirit and attitude which was evidenced in the revolt against England in 1776.

A similar prototype of the revolution would be the well-known Boston Tea Party of December 16, 1773. Here a number of the colonists of Massachusetts took matters in their own hands in order to convince the British that they could not put arbitrary taxes on goods shipped to the American colonies.

As the revolution is used to assess the importance of events before 1776, it also gives meaning to events which came later. For example, the meaning of the Emancipation Proclamation of Abraham Lincoln is explained by historians in terms of the freedoms which were guaranteed to all citizens when our nation was founded. Similarly, the Women's Suffrage

Movement of a more recent date is understood in terms of an extension of the democratic principles involved in the revolution. It may be that future historians will regard the Civil Rights Bill of 1964 as a dramatic symbol of the principles involved in the founding of our nation.

Now that we have seen how a typology of history works in terms of American history, let us apply the same principle to biblical history. Obviously, the central event which gives meaning to all other biblical events is Jesus Christ. For purposes of this discussion let us consider the "revelation of God in Christ" as being one event. This will spare us a lengthy discussion as to which of the elements in the life, death, and resurrection of our Lord is the most significant. The important factor at this point is that we have a certain understanding of God in terms of the totality of his revelation through his Son.

When we understand Christ as the crucial event in biblical history, giving meaning to all other events, we see that the Exodus-Wilderness experience described in the books of Exodus and Numbers becomes a prototype of the Christ event. It shows God's concern for his people and his willingness to involve himself in their history on their behalf. By the same token, we see in Hosea's experience with his wife and his declaration of the love of God on the basis of that experience a prototype of God's act in Christ. We find in the preaching of Hosea the same divine love which we find represented by Jesus Christ.

45

Looking at the biblical account of the period after the resurrection of our Lord, we see the death of Stephen and the life and ministry of the apostle Paul as post-types of the Christ event. In both cases the witnesses of these men find their meaning in terms of the revelation of God in Christ. Apart from an understanding of Christology, neither the death of Stephen nor the activity of Paul makes any sense.

If we continue to examine church history beyond the biblical period, we find a number of post-types of the Christ event in every century. Protestants would point to the Reformation as a posttype of the Christ event, insofar as it involved a return to the basic principles of the New Testament. Similarly, we might point to the Aldersgate experience of John Wesley, which finds its meaning and importance only in terms of a correct understanding of God's act in Christ.[24]

But we must remember that our interpretation of biblical history as Christology is acceptable only to those who are in the Christian tradition. A Jewish theologian would deny that Christ is the central point of history, dividing all of biblical history into "before" and "after." He would point to the event of the Exodus and the covenant with Moses on Mount Sinai as being the crucial events of the biblical story. Then the covenant of God with Abraham would be seen as a prototype of the Exodus-Covenant event, and the victory of the Maccabees over the Seleucids

46

would be seen as a post-type. For the Christian, the Christ event is the climax of the entire Old Testament. For the Jew, the Old Testament *contains* the climax of biblical revelation, and the Christ event is simply an interesting theological dead end.

Since as Christians we are committed to a christological view of the Old Testament, we must read its pages in that light. In dealing with Old Testament material we accept those things which agree with our understanding of what God has done in Christ. We reject those things which apparently contradict this knowledge.

With this theological yardstick in mind, let us go back to the Old Testament and see what it says to us concerning the act of God on behalf of man and the needs of man which are met by these acts. In reading the Old Testament in terms of Christian typology, we find that a great deal of it seems very much up to date and very challenging to us. It speaks eloquently to the needs which we have in our own personal life today. It also speaks very clearly to certain community, national, and international situations which are giving us trouble.

When we look at the Book of Amos, for example, we see that nearly all the concerns of this prophet, which he described in terms of his own day, are paralleled very closely in our own daily newspapers. Amos speaks of the oppression of the poor on the part of the rich. He describes the robbery of those who are unable to defend themselves from unscrupulous

47

politicians and court officials. He denounces his people for the lawlessness and violence going on in the streets. He describes in some detail the inhuman treatment which some groups of men are using to crush others, both at home and around the world. He describes the idolatry of his day, which takes the form of the worship of idols and forces of nature rather than God himself.

Almost every word which Amos uttered speaks as forcefully and personally to our society, and to us as individuals, as in Amos' own day. We can recognize in our society all the problems which he dealt with. The business of idolatry may give us momentary pause. Certainly, in our day and age men do not worship metal idols, nor do they make sacrifices to trees, plants, and shrubs. Or do they?

Several years ago I was living in a city on the east coast and preaching every Sunday morning in a town some twenty-five miles away. In order to get to church on Sunday, I had to drive through about ten miles of typical American suburbia. Traveling the same route week after week, I became aware of certain habits in the behavior of the American suburbanite on Sunday morning. Relatively few of the people whose homes I passed attended church. Most of them spent Sunday morning in their front yards. Week after week I was able to observe certain rituals peculiar to various residents. One man could always be counted on to be washing and polishing his Cadillac from 10:00 A.M. until noon. Another invariably spent Sunday morning grooming his convertible. A third could always be found on his hands and knees on the front lawn, searching for stray weeds which had crept into his prized turf during the past week. Another usually spent the whole morning fertilizing and pruning the shrubs and rose bushes in his yard.

It seems to me that these are perfect examples of pagan idolatry, exactly equivalent to that of Amos' day. These people had no sense of responsibility to God. They never took the trouble to attend a service of worship on Sunday morning. Their attention was directed not toward God but to the symbols of their material wealth and social status. The shiny automobile in the driveway was just as much a metal idol as a golden calf. The ritual involving the front lawn and the rose bushes is very similar to the worship of the fertility Baals of an olive orchard. In the time of Amos people turned away from God and committed idolatry by putting their trust in things. In our own day material goods which represent our social status have put their claim upon our time, take the money which we would otherwise be using for religious and charitable purposes, and have become the things which give meaning to our lives. In spite of the fact that we can consider ourselves to be a civilized and sophisticated people, we have not progressed beyond the idolatry of the eighth century B.C.

When we read the words of Amos or the other ethical sections of the Old Testament, we become

49

acutely aware of the message which these men of old have for our day. The denunciations of evil, injustice, and selfishness which were made five hundred or one thousand years before Christ are just as timely today as they were then. And we must recognize the fact that an awareness of the needs of our society and the answers to those needs which are found in the Old Testament constitutes a challenge to action on our part.

The sixth chapter of Isaiah illustrates the fact that an awareness of God's plan and man's need is a call to action. As Isaiah worshiped in the temple one day, he became aware of the presence of God before him. He stared at the vision of God and marveled at his righteousness, purity, and holiness. Then he looked at himself and shrank back in horror when he realized how imperfect and insignificant he was. Furthermore, he recognized the fact that his uncleanness was shared by his entire generation. As he beheld the purity of God and contrasted it with his own sinfulness and weakness, he asked himself, "Who will go to tell the people what I have seen here today?" In the silence which followed, Isaiah realized that his awareness of the need for a prophet was in fact a call for him to become one. Therefore, because he had seen the will of God and the need of man, he volunteered himself, saying, "Here I am, Lord, send me."

When we see the message of the Old Testament in terms of the needs of our society today, we receive a similar call to go forth as prophets. But as we do so, we must be faithful to the revelation of God as it is found in Jesus Christ. Any social action which we must undertake must be theologically sound in terms of our doctrine of Christ.

Since we have an awareness of the need for twentieth-century prophets to deal with the problems of our society, we must discover a theologically sound basis for using the New Testament witness of God's will and the Old Testament witness interpreted in the light of the New. What is the basis on which we should go forth into the world? How can we be sure that we will make an authentic witness, as we attempt to apply God's word to man's need? In order to answer that question, we must look at the theological and biblical basis of social action in the past. Only when we understand where the Protestant church has been, in social action, can we understand the demands of the present situation. And in order to see the beginnings of social action in Protestantism, we must begin with the situation facing the church in the eighteenth century.

4

Deists, Calvinists, and
Wesley

Protestantism of the eighteenth century had little
concern for what we refer to today as "Christian social action." There was no tradition of concern for
social problems handed down from the Reformation.
Neither of the two leading figures of the Reformation period was much interested in the social problems which had robbed men of life, liberty, justice,
health, and peace of mind. Martin Luther's magnifi-
cent theological insights did little to enlighten his
social views. Politically and economically he was
committed to a medieval feudalism which did little
to lessen the social problems of his day.[25] His attitude can be seen in his refusal to side with the German peasants in their rebellion against their feudal
overlords. The theology of John Calvin, as we shall
see shortly, did little to lead to a concern for social
problems and their remedies, at least for several
centuries.

If the heritage of the Reformation provided little
basis for Christian social action in the eighteenth
century, the main philosophical and religious cur-

rents of the day provided even less. One of the dominant theological positions of the day was *deism,* which had linked arms with the philosophy known as rationalism.

The God of the deists was sometimes referred to as "the Divine Watchmaker." It was assumed that God did exist and that he was the creator of the universe. But after he created the world, he ordained an unchangeable set of rules and regulations to govern its every need and then set it off by itself in a corner of creation, to run on its own. Since he had created divine laws to govern every aspect of the universe, there was no necessity for him to have anything further to do with it or with the men who lived in it. Therefore there was no direct communication or relationship between the Creator and his creation.

This deistic view of God had a profound effect on a theological view of society. All human interaction was thought to be governed by the unchangeable rules which God had ordained. Generally speaking, things were just about the way that God had intended them to be. He had created justice and injustice, wealth and poverty, health and illness, happiness and misery. If left to themselves, all these factors would interact with one another in terms of God's laws, and the total outcome would be good. All the situations which existed in society, since they had been created by God, must be in accordance with his will. Therefore there was no desire to change anything. Men should not interfere with things which

God had arranged. Neither should they question the wisdom of the Creator in making things as they were.

The only appropriate action of men and the Christian church, in terms of society, was to leave things alone so that God's laws could work themselves out. If anything really went wrong and a situation became intolerable, it was thought that this was because of the meddling of ill-advised men. Therefore men should not pass laws controlling political and economic processes in any way. These would simply interfere with the laws which God had provided to govern society. Wherever such meddling human laws had been passed, it was the responsibility of the Christian to see that they were repealed before they did any more damage. The political and economic theory which derives from this belief is known as *laissez faire,* a French term meaning "let it alone." [26]

Of course deism was not normative orthodox Christianity. It was combined with the philosophy of rationalism, which tended to eliminate most of the "supernatural" or "superstitious" elements from the Christian faith. Well, what of the orthodox Christians in the eighteenth century? Weren't they able to counter the lack of concern for social problems among the deists?

Unfortunately the dominant element in Protestant Orthodoxy in the eighteenth century was Calvinism. And one of the dominant doctrines of Calvinism is that of Predestination. Except for some Presbyterians, there are very few Protestants who know what Calvin meant by Predestination.[27] An often repeated story which illustrates the most common misunderstanding of Predestination is that of the Presbyterian minister who fell down the cellar stairs. Landing at the bottom, he recovered his senses, got to his feet, dusted himself off, and said, "Well, thank goodness that's over with!" This story may be humorous, but it is unfair to the Presbyterians. Predestination does not mean that God has worked out detailed plans for everything which cannot be changed. It does not mean that what is going to happen to you tomorrow has already been prearranged.

The doctrine of Predestination means simply that some people have been destined, from the beginning of time, for salvation and some people have not. This doctrine is based on a somewhat selective reading of Paul's letter to the Romans, especially chap. 8, vss. 28-30. Inasmuch as God had chosen some people for salvation and had eliminated others, the eighteenth-century Calvinist looked within himself and others for "signs of election" which would show the evidence of God's favor and grace. Prosperity, health, and happiness were looked upon as being evidences of election. On the other hand poverty, disease, inability to hold a job, and inability to cope with life were looked upon as signs of divine disfavor. Therefore there was no reason to try to improve the situation of those who could not get along on their own. Why should good Christians who showed all the signs of divine favor and election concern themselves with the miseries of those whose problems clearly indicated that God had rejected them? [28] Calvin was interested in social problems, such as "pauperism," but his solution was to admonish those in need to get busy and support themselves. Calvinism attempted to influence every aspect of life, but the emphasis was invariably on individual morality and righteousness, not on social problems per se.

Thus we see that the deism of left-wing Protestantism and the strict Calvinism of orthodox Protestantism both tended to lead men away from a sense of responsibility for Christian social concern. In the middle of the eighteenth century there was little emphasis on social reform among English and European Protestants.

The Church of England was no exception. Within its structure the effects of both deism and Calvinism could be seen quite clearly. Although these two points of view were far apart theologically, each one had a strong group of adherents within the Anglican communion. Furthermore, in the Church of England there was a third factor which tended to blunt the social conscience of the church. This might be called *institutionalism*. The Church of England was supported by the government and had very little contact with the people. Because it was not dependent upon contributions from its members but was supported by a church tax, the church could exist as an institution without any approval or support from its parishioners. In the mid-eighteenth century, the Anglican Church had very little influence on the life of the nation. Services were held regularly in the churches, and the sacrament of the Lord's Supper was provided, but very few people bothered to take advantage of either. Those who did attend church, largely on special occasions, were the upper classes. The church had little or no contact with, nor interest in, people who worked for a living. Its leaders were concerned only in perpetuating the institution, so that an unbroken historical succession would continue.

Few churches have had less social concern or evangelical fervor than the eighteenth-century Church of England. And yet it was this very church which gave birth to the Wesleyan revival. But John Wesley was by no means a typical Anglican of his day. During the course of his ministry, he rebelled against each one of the factors which we have already discussed.

During Wesley's student days at Oxford, he became impatient with the deism and rationalism of his teachers and his colleagues. He and a small group of friends became quite conspicuous among the ministerial students at Oxford, because they attended worship regularly and received communion frequently. He could not accept the notion of a God who had created a world and then deserted it, but felt that God was an active force in the world day by day. As he studied the orthodoxy of his day, he was equally appalled by the strict Calvinism which he encountered. He could not reconcile his understanding of divine love and the forgiving grace of God with the notion that some people had been predestined for damnation from the beginning of time. Thus neither deism nor Calvinism blunted Wesley's awareness of both the spiritual and the social needs of the English people of his day. After his "heartwarming experience" in Aldersgate Street in 1738, he went out to meet both sets of his peoples' needs. He preached with an evangelistic zeal which fitted in well with the spirit of the New Testament. But it sounded very strange indeed in Anglican pulpits. The rich and well-born people who heard him preach in their churches were shocked at what he said. They could not bring themselves to believe that the people who worked in coal mines had any claim on the interest and concern of God. Certainly, if God was interested in anyone it was only in the upper classes! [29] It was not long before Wesley's enthusiasm caused the leaders of the Anglican Church to bar him from their pulpits. Eventually there was not a single preaching place in the Church of England which was open to him.

But one of Wesley's fellow workers in the revival which he was starting had already found a solution to that problem. George Whitefield had left the ornate pulpits of beautiful churches and was preaching in the poorest sections of England to coal miners in the fields.[30] He soon convinced Wesley that preaching in the open air and in public buildings was the only way to spread the gospel in England. To the amazement and dismay of the Anglican Church, the Wesleyan revival spread across England. The Wesleys and their followers were not content merely to preach the Christian gospel to anyone who would listen. They also were concerned about the many social problems which were grinding men down into the dirt of the slums. The forces of the new Methodist "societies" were mobilized to help people who could not help themselves. Food was taken to those who were going hungry. Clothing was provided for those who had been dressed in rags. Methodist preachers and class leaders went into prisons to serve the spiritual and physical needs of the prisoners. Even hardened criminals who had been condemned to death were not considered to be beyond the grace of God or the concern of the church. Both John and Charles Wesley rode to the gallows with condemned murderers and stayed by their sides, praying with them until they had been executed. The conditions in jails of that period were unbelievably bad. Prisoners lived in filth and squalor. Jailers received no salaries but lived on bribes taken from the prisoners. The attention which the early Methodists focused upon these problems was one of the factors in the general prison reform which took place in England later in the century.

John Wesley was very much concerned with the poverty and misery of the lower classes in general. Money was provided from the treasuries of his societies to help the poor survive their hardships. Schools were founded in which the children could learn to read, so that they would be able to improve their condition. An attempt was made to provide medical care for those who were weakened by disease. Wesley and his followers attacked the widespread use of liquor, especially cheap gin, as a means of escape from the realities of slum living. One particularly bad social evil which was fought by the Methodists was the institution of slavery. Wesley denounced the slave trade more bitterly than any other practice of his day. Those who joined his societies were forbidden to hold slaves or to buy, sell, or transport them.[31] Before the century ended, the opposition to slavery which had arisen largely out of his concern found its way into Parliament, and the institution was outlawed.[32]

With the Wesleyan revival we see the dawning of a new day in Christian evangelism. The early Methodists had a tremendous evangelistic fervor and allowed nothing to stop them from winning men to Christ. On the other hand they realized that Christian concern could not stop with a man's soul. If the church was really concerned about society, it had to do something about the dehumanizing factors in English social life. Unfortunately the major concern of Wesley and his followers was the plight of the individual rather than the social system which had caused the trouble in the first place. For this reason the Methodists tended to treat *symptoms* of social problems rather than the diseases themselves. But most of the sweeping social changes which took place at the end of the eighteenth century were brought about by political leaders who had had their consciences sensitized by the Methodist revival.[33]

The effects of Wesley's revival in England and in the United States can scarcely be overemphasized. Historians have even suggested that Wesley and his followers saved England from a blood bath similar to the French Revolution of 1789.[34] The work that Wesley began in England did not remain there but spread both to the continent and to the newly established colonies in North America. As the eighteenth century drew to a close, it appeared that Methodism had set the stage for a new concept in Christian service. A fervent evangelism was balanced with a clear and powerful social concern. But the nineteenth century was to bring new theological developments, which were to drive a wedge of division between evangelism and social concern.

5

Social Action—and Reaction

In order to understand the development of Protestant theology in the nineteenth and early twentieth centuries, we must take a look at a number of new forces which were at work in reshaping nineteenth-century culture. One of the most important factors was a change in the way in which history was viewed, called "historicism." Historicism is another fancy name for a very simple concept. History had previously been seen primarily as a series of events, or a series of movements. Historicism, which grew partly out of the romanticism of the nineteenth century, said that the basic unit of history was man himself. The basic subject matter of history was now viewed as human life in all its varied complex aspects.[35]

Coupled with the human interest of historicism was a new scientific method which was now being applied to the writing of history. During the preceding century a great many new tools had become available to the historians for reconstructing the past in detail. Large numbers of ancient written records had been found in various parts of the world, giving to the historian a tremendous new source of material.[36] Furthermore a number of ancient languages had now been deciphered for the first time.[37] Because of these two developments it was now possible to read through the entire library of an ancient king of Babylonia, Assyria, or Egypt. Previously history had largely been dependent upon secondary sources for the stories of what these kings had done.

At the same time archaeology was beginning to develop as a science.[38] It was discovered that there were valuable clues to the past hidden in the soil of the ancient Near East. Scholars began excavating at the sites of ancient cities, and little by little the examination and analysis of the materials found began to develop scientifically.[39] On the basis of all these new resources and techniques, historians began to view themselves as scientists. It was now thought by many historians that a complete reconstruction of all the important events of the past was only a matter of time and patient hard work.

The change which took place in history was paralleled by a change in the way in which literature was viewed. Because of new discoveries and broadening of scholarly interests, a very wide selection of world literature was now available for comparative studies. As these studies were made, it was seen that certain patterns could be identified and charted. On the basis of these patterns and new developments in historical and literary method, procedures were developed for tracing literary units to their sources and evaluating the sources in terms of historical validity. At the same time work was begun on oral traditions and folk literature. The first work which was done along this line focused on German folk literature. But before very long, the scientific study of literature handed down in oral form moved to the Old Testament, and then to the New Testament.[40]

One of the most startling features of the eighteenth century was the tremendous development of modern science. During the eighteenth century new discoveries worked complete revolutions in mathematics, astronomy, chemistry, biology, and medicine. At the very end of the eighteenth century, James Hutton[41] published a book entitled *The Theory of the Earth*. In this work he stated that the geological processes changing the earth today are approximately the same as those of bygone ages. This means that the development of the present form of the world has been a slow and regular process. On the basis of Hutton's study of rocks, scientists began to develop a new science known as geology. And this new science, aided by new discoveries in other fields, began to challenge the biblical story of creation. Now it appeared that the world was not created in its present form in a few days but had developed over a period of perhaps millions of years.

It was no longer possible for theology to ignore science. As the nineteenth century progressed, more and more scientific theories and experimental data seemed to challenge many of the statements in the

64

Bible, both in the Old and New Testaments. Science had a tremendous hold upon the intellectual class, because so many of its theories seemed to come to life in the laboratory before the eyes of the observer. The time had come when a confrontation between science and religion was unavoidable.

The theologians of the nineteenth century had two choices. On the one hand they could denounce science and all its discoveries as being anti-Christian and incorrect. In doing so they would alienate not only the men of science but most of the other educated people of their culture as well. This would rob the church of the kind of intellectual leadership that it would need if it was to keep its place in society. It would also reduce the opportunity of the church to preach the Christian gospel. The only alternative seemed to be to enter into dialogue with science. In this way the Bible would be opened to all the investigations of history, literary analysis, and science. Biblical scholars would join with scientists, historians, and literary experts in analyzing the material which was in the Bible, to assess its real meaning and worth. In the encounter it might be necessary to give up or change some of the things which had been a part of the Christian tradition for generations. On the other hand, if the Bible really was worth anything, it would not be demolished by science but would come through the encounter unharmed. Whatever was left after scientific, literary, and historical analysis had finished would be the very essence of the Christian faith, which would then be preached to and accepted by all mankind. An openness to this kind of encounter was, of course, the decision which was finally made.[42]

Another factor in the intellectual development of the nineteenth century which turned out to be very important for Protestant theology was the philosophy of Hegel.[43] The most significant element of Hegel's theology was his theory of dialectic. The dialectical process was the interaction of opposing ideas or philosophies. Hegel said that every *thesis* or idea is inevitably opposed by an *antithesis*. Out of the dialogue (hence the name dialectic) which takes place between the thesis and the antithesis comes a new idea called a *synthesis*. This synthesis replaces both of the original theses. Because it preserves the best of the thesis and the antithesis, it is a higher and better idea than either of its predecessors. However, the synthesis immediately becomes a new thesis. As such it is opposed by *its* opposite notion or antithesis. The new thesis and antithesis interact with one another to bring forth a new synthesis. This, in turn, becomes a new thesis, and so the process goes on indefinitely. The result of all this is, of course, that ideas keep getting more and more perfect. As the dialectical process continues, there is an inevitable progress. Man keeps getting better and better, and so does the society in which he lives. The cycle of progress is inevitable.

The final item which we should note among the

new forces that work in the nineteenth century is the development of social science. Out of the successes of physical and biological sciences came a determination to apply the scientific method to social phenomena. Students of culture noted that there were certain patterns in society just as in phenomena of nature. If it was possible to list and describe natural phenomena and then conduct experiments to discover physical laws, why would it not be possible to experiment with society in such a way as to discover the laws of social interaction? The development of social science was much slower than that of natural science, but it was noted that there were certain patterns of cause and effect in human interaction, and that on the basis of these patterns it was sometimes possible to alter social situations by changing certain factors in the structure of society.

So much for a quick analysis of some of the new factors at work in the nineteenth century. Our question now is, "What is the importance of all these new developments in terms of the situation in theology?" One of the leading themes of nineteenth-century Protestant theology was the "quest for the historic Jesus." This was partly a result of the emphasis on human life of historicism, which insisted that the life of Jesus was of tremendous importance in understanding the development of Christianity. At the same time scientific historiography insisted that it was possible to reconstruct the life of Jesus with some precision. All that was necessary was an appli-

67

cation of the new methods of historical research and literary analysis to the Gospel accounts and other contemporary literature. When this was done, a clear and unmistakable picture of the real Jesus of Nazareth would shine forth. A number of people attempted to draw a verbal picture of the historical Jesus. Today we can see that these pictures differed considerably from one scholar to another. On the other hand there are certain common factors which are found in nearly all of them.[44]

All the interpreters of the historical Jesus agreed that Jesus of Nazareth was a man with a mission. He had dedicated himself to the mission, and nothing swayed him from his determination to accomplish it. On the other hand it was generally agreed that the mission of Jesus had been badly misunderstood by Christian theologians through the years. The simple, straightforward interests of Jesus had been distorted by nineteen hundred years of theology into an unrecognizable form. The difficulty arose from an overemphasis upon supernaturalism. The Gospel writers had introduced a number of foreign supernatural elements into the story of Jesus. The apostle Paul had misunderstood Jesus completely and had tried to turn him into a theologian. For this reason Jesus had appeared through the ages as a worker of miracles who spoke about salvation and who looked forward to the end of world history in the final judgment in the near future.

The science and philosophy of the nineteenth century had helped to show theologians how incorrect this picture of Jesus really was. On the basis of these new disciplines and new ideas, however, it would be possible to restore the original Jesus to his first-century simplicity. However, this meant that a number of elements in the Gospel stories had to be removed. On the basis of current knowledge it was obvious that both the virgin-birth stories and the idea of a preexistent Logos, found in the Fourth Gospel, were indefensible. Jesus of Nazareth was only a *man*. The doctrine of the Incarnation was considered to be an unimportant theological development of the intervening years. Similarly the emphasis in the preaching of Jesus on salvation was a misreading of his real purpose and intention. By the same token the concern with the end of the world and the final judgment must have been placed in the mouth of Jesus by later interpreters. On the basis of these assumptions, the supernatural elements in the story of Jesus were stripped away, one by one.

What remained after the job had been completed? One element in Jesus' ministry shone like a polished diamond amid the wreckage of the gospel traditions. This was the ethical preaching of Jesus. Nowhere before in world literature had anyone seen a set of ethics which surpassed those of the Sermon on the Mount! A second factor which remained was the interest of Jesus in the "kingdom of God." It had previously been thought that the kingdom of God had something to do with the end of this world and the dawning of the new age. Now the concern with such things had been removed as an element in Jesus' preaching. But it was impossible to get rid of all his references to the kingdom of God. Therefore it must have had a different meaning for Jesus. Finally it was decided that the kingdom of God meant "the world as God really wants it to be."

Now it was possible to combine the ethical preaching of Jesus and his interest in the kingdom of God. The task of the Christian, therefore, was to bring about the kingdom of God. And the kingdom of God was no equivalent to a perfect society. This placed upon the Christian church a heavy responsibility for social action. Certainly God never intended people to be poor, hungry, ignorant, and diseased. It was obvious that man's knowledge of social processes and social science had come along just in time to enable the Christian to remake society as God wanted it to be.

In the light of this situation the social action plan of Protestantism swiftly took shape. By 1900, the theology of "liberalism" or "modernism" had spread from Europe to the United States.[45] The United States offered a fertile field for the growth of what came to be known as the "social gospel." The country was only a century and a quarter old. Vast areas of it were just being settled. Industries and utilities were growing at a fantastic rate. Those who had the shrewdness to be in the right place at the right time, and the strength to fight off competitors, became the owners of vast financial empires. It was the age of big business. The country's net worth rose at a fantastic rate. But the bulk of the money was quickly gathered into the hands of a relatively few men. With a few notable exceptions the new industrial tycoons and railroad barons had no concern for the welfare of the men whose labor made their fortunes possible.

Slums grew and festered in all large cities. Graft and corruption flourished openly from coast to coast. Public health programs seemed to be a lost cause. Factory employees tried to organize into labor unions for collective bargaining with employers but had little success.[46]

It was obvious that there were many situations which needed correction. Conditions which made it possible for some men to grow rich made it impossible for others to survive. The new social gospel of the church had answers for at least some of these problems.[47] The Christian church felt a responsibility to come to the aid of the helpless. But it was now obvious that simply relieving the suffering of individuals was not enough. That was treating symptoms instead of curing the disease itself. It was necessary to treat social ills by the proper use of political power and economic pressures.

There were some people who shrank away from the idea of the church becoming involved in politics. How could this be reconciled with the separation which Jesus implied in his statement about God and Caesar? [48] But the leaders in the social gospel movement cited biblical precedents for their involvement. The question a Christian has to ask himself, they insisted, is, "What would Jesus have done in this situation?" And Jesus had been very much involved in relieving the suffering of the unfortunate.

Jesus had healed the sick. He had fed the poor. He had denounced the rich who lived in luxury and ignored the suffering of the poor. Obviously the Christian should do likewise. Jesus was opposed to the use of violence. Therefore the Christian should be a pacifist. Jesus and his disciples owned nothing as individuals, but each contributed what he had to a fund which provided for the needs of all.[49] Some saw in this the basis for an equalitarian system of socialism.

The best-known name among the spokesmen for the social gospel was Walter Rauschenbusch. After serving as a Baptist pastor in New York City, he taught for some twenty years at Rochester Theological Seminary, a center of theological liberalism in the East. The influence of Rauschenbusch and his colleagues in the social gospel movement spread far and wide. Across the nation young pastors went forth to lead in the battle for social and economic equality for all citizens. But the church as a whole was not yet ready to follow its leaders in social action. Many of the young crusading pastors were warned to modify their views or leave the church. Some trimmed their sails for the time being. Others regretfully left the church and took their concerns into the arena of politics on a full-time basis. One of the latter was a young Presbyterian minister named Norman Thomas who was in later years several times a candidate for president on the socialist ticket. Although denounced at the time as a dangerous radical, he has lived to see most of his original concerns incorporated into the platforms of both leading political parties.[50]

The social gospel movement succeeded in making the gospel relevant to the needs of society. But it had paid a high price for doing so. The doctrine of the Incarnation had been replaced by the figure of a teacher of ethics. The grace of God had been crowded out by the inevitability of progress and the belief that man could work out his own collective salvation.

It is not surprising that liberalism and the social gospel evoked a violent backlash within Protestantism. There were many who did not take kindly to the anti-supernaturalism of the new tradition which was a radical departure from classical orthodoxy. They saw that the attempt to come to terms with the challenge of modern science, history, and literary analysis had resulted in a radical change in confessional theology.

One wing of the Protestant church decided, on the basis of this evidence, that all modern science and scholarship were irrelevant and dangerous to the Christian faith. The only way to protect the Christian faith from being eviscerated was to return to

73

the atmosphere of the past, in which it had been relatively safe. Modern science was seen as a satanic temptation, designed to lure faithful Christians away from the biblical truth. What was needed was a return to the fundamentals of the faith; hence the name "fundamentalism." [51]

The fundamentalists insisted upon the absolute accuracy of the Bible. If it was valid theologically, it was also valid scientifically. Instead of actually returning to biblical fundamentals, this movement turned back to Protestant scholasticism.[52] In this system the Bible was absolutely infallible and so was *any* theological statement which could be deduced logically *from* the Bible. This, of course, opened the door to the promoting of all sorts of strange ideas as absolute dogma.

Modernism was one of the chief targets of fundamentalism. Anything which had been said or done under that banner was wrong. The rules of navigation for fundamentalist theology were very simple: just set your compass 180° from liberal theology and proceed at full speed! Since liberals had opened the Bible to the challenge of science and historical research, the fundamentalists slammed it shut. Then they very carefully built around the Bible a fence which was, in the picturesque language of my Arkansan students, "bull-strong, hog-tight, and deer-high." The Bible was effectively sealed off from corruption by the world. But a fence is not a one-way valve! And the Bible, thus protected, had no chance to transform the modern world.

For the fundamentalists this was not a cause· for concern. Social action was not a proper function for the church. Let society take care of itself! The task of the church was the saving of souls. Religion was seen as a stable, unchanging element in a changing world. It was a *personal* matter, the relationship of the individual with God. Ethics were important, yes, but on a *personal* basis. The moral questions for fundamentalism were those which involved personal ethical decisions. Oddly enough, the question asked of the Bible was the same question asked by the liberal: "What would Jesus have done?" But the frame of reference was quite different. Jesus would obviously not have smoked, used liquor, danced, played cards, or attended the theater. The Christian was therefore to be tested by whether or not he did these things.

Some Protestant denominations included within their ranks leading social gospelists and fundamentalists. During the heyday of American liberalism and social concern, for example, many influential Methodist pulpits shook with the thunder of the social gospel. But when the fundamentalist reaction set in, many Methodist pietists were in the vanguard.

This tended to split denominations into two camps. On the one hand you had the liberals or modernists, who had a strong social conscience but refused to become concerned over the fine points of theology. In the other camp were the fundamental-ists. They were very much concerned, and rightly so, with the preservation of the basic tenets of ortho-dox Christianity. On the other hand social action was denounced by this group, largely because of its relationship with liberalism.[53] The fundamentalists saw that the liberals, in a very real sense, had thrown the baby out with the bathwater. They were deter-mined never to let this happen again. Therefore they made a decision that no bathwater should ever be thrown away in the future!

As a result of this bitter feud, social action in American Protestantism was in a desperate situation. The only choice was social concern with little theo-logical foundation, or an orthodox theology which had no concept of social responsibility. Unfortu-nately, even in Methodist circles, the Wesleyan tradition of combining evangelical orthodoxy with a lively social concern was lost in the noise and dust of battle.

Until the time of World War II, the two choices outlined above were the only options which seemed available to churchmen. There were many noble attempts to break these stereotypes and to show that social action is not an either-or type of thing, which involves a rejection of theological integrity. But once an idea is firmly ingrained, it is very difficult to change it.

Recently in a Kansas City restaurant I ran across an example of the mental set which I have been describing. I was sitting with a theological student, listening to his explanation of a problem with which he was struggling. The woman in the next booth overheard our conversation and leaned over to ask what my religious affiliation was. I told her that I was a Methodist minister and a teacher in a theological seminary. At once her eyes gleamed and her mouth set in a hard firm line. "Aha!" she exclaimed, "then you are one of those modernists." I tried to reassure her that it was not necessary to be a modernist in order to be a Methodist professor. But she as a member of an interdenominational Bible fellowship church knew better than that! A tiny, knowing smile played about her lips all the time I was talking. She insisted that in order to understand the meaning of the Christian faith you must be concerned with evangelism. I agreed. Then I changed the direction of the conversation a bit and invited her to attend an evangelistic mission to be held in Kansas City, featuring the Australian evangelist, Alan Walker. She was absolutely delighted to hear that there was still a Methodist minister of some prominence who was serving as an evangelist. Her eyes simply glowed as she exclaimed, "Well! He must be one of those old-fashioned shouting Methodists, who still believes in the Bible!"

As far as the layman is concerned, this has been precisely the dilemma of normative Protestantism for too long. Everyone is categorized as either a social actionist and therefore "far-out" theologically, or an "old-fashioned shouting Evangelist" who is concerned only about personal religion. The time has come to break out of this stereotyped mold. The theological groundwork has long since been laid for a deep and abiding social concern which is also thoroughly evangelistic in nature and theologically sound. But this understanding has not yet filtered into the places where it can do the most good. We recognize the need for both a strong vital evangelistic faith and for a social conscience which will lead us forth to help work out the will of God in society. Let us see, then, what might be the biblical and theological foundation for such a mission!

6

The Gospel for Today

In the liberal movement American Protestantism had seen a great need for social action. It was recognized that poverty, disease, ignorance, and oppression were contrary to the will of God and had to be eliminated. Furthermore the leaders of this movement saw that the church itself had a responsibility to act in these situations. As long as human rights and human dignity were being denied, the church of Jesus Christ could not stand by as an idle spectator.

The social gospel movement was able to accomplish a great deal in the way of Christian social action. The problems which were attacked were serious and needed some attention. Although the solutions offered by social gospelists were by no means perfect, most of the social reforms of the twentieth century can be found reflected in the concerns and the programs of Walter Rauschenbusch and other theologians of the period.

However, when we view the entire panorama of modernism and the social gospel from the perspective of our own day, we can see certain basic errors which were made. The situation of those who answered the call of the social gospel movement might be likened to that of the young Samuel.

I Samuel 3 contains the story of Samuel's call to be a prophet. As he was sleeping in his accustomed place in the temple one night, he was awakened by a voice which called him to action. He realized that this was a call which must be obeyed, and so he ran to Eli, the priest of the temple, to see what was wanted. But Eli had not called the boy. So Samuel returned to his place and once again fell asleep. A second time the same call came to him. Once again he ran to Eli to see what was wanted. Once again he was told to lie down in his place. Then the entire scene was repeated a third time. Finally Eli realized that the call must have come to Samuel from God himself. He told the boy to return once again to his place and wait for the call to come once more. The next time it came, his response should be, "Speak, Lord, for thy servant is listening." Samuel was so anxious to answer the call to service, that he had run three times in the wrong direction before finding out what was required in the way of an answer.

And so it was with the social gospel movement. An urgent call was heard, and it was answered quickly and conscientiously. By some standards the answer was the one which was needed. And yet, in another sense, the answer of the social gospel was as much "off course" as was the response of Samuel. For in the process of making an extremely helpful social witness the church had its theological foundations very badly weakened. And in a real sense, what was given away in the process was even more vital than what was gained.

The liberalism which characterized the last half of the nineteenth century and the first decades of the twentieth has largely run its course and disappeared. It is true that there are many theologians today who cling proudly to the heritage of theological liberalism. But the liberalism which they espouse has undergone a great many changes because of the theological developments of the last forty years. In mainline Protestantism, nineteenth-century liberalism has largely lost its threat today. And the reason that this has happened can be found in the inadequacy of many of the central doctrines of that position.[54]

One of the major problems of this type of liberalism was what we must consider today to be its inadequate Christology. The doctrine of the Incarnation is too central to the Christian faith to be dispensed with as an unnecessary hangover from first-century supernaturalism. Without this doctrine Jesus Christ becomes simply a teacher who gave us an excellent example of ethical living and a number of admirable sermons and then met a tragic death. This removes the theological core of the Christian faith and reduces the church to a society for the preservation of ethical humanism.

A second theological problem of liberalism was its

dependence upon the reconstruction of the historic Jesus. In 1900, Albert Schweitzer published a book entitled *The Quest for the Historic Jesus.*[55] He surveyed all the attempts which had been made to recover the facts of the life of Jesus and to write a biography of Jesus in terms of nineteenth-century standards. He showed conclusively that no one of the lives of Jesus which had been written was adequate, and went on to explain clearly why the attempt itself was hopeless. The effect of his book was to demolish the foundation upon which the search for the "Jesus of history" had rested. His arguments were conclusive. History has shown that he was indeed a prophet. But his words were not really taken to heart by theologians in Germany until after World War I, and another twenty years passed before his influence was felt in the United States.

Schweitzer showed that we can never recover Jesus exactly as he was in the first century. Actually all the pictures of Jesus which had been found by well-meaning biblical scholars turned out to be distorted mirror-images of their own ideas and prejudices. For example, the theologians of the nineteenth century had proved to their own satisfaction that Jesus had no real interest in eschatology, i.e., in a study of the end of the world and the final judgment. They showed quite conclusively that all the eschatological passages attributed to Jesus were in fact placed in his mouth by later theologians. In the latter part of his book Schweitzer showed that the lack of concern with "the final things" which characterized nineteenth-century theologians was not shared by Jesus. All the evidence seems to show that Jesus' teachings about the final things are among the most authentic statements that we have in the New Testament.

The point which Schweitzer made is one which must be taken very seriously by theologians today. Inasmuch as we can never recover an exact knowledge of who Jesus was or what he thought, the question, "What would Jesus have done in this situation?" is a useless and nearly meaningless one. This statement has tremendous theological significance, because *this was the question which was asked both by the liberal social gospelist and the fundamentalist as well.* But now if we are going to use the Bible as a basis for Christian living, we must take a *different* question to the New Testament. All that the New Testament can tell us is what kind of God it is who would enter personally into human history, in the life, death, and resurrection of Jesus Christ. On this basis we can come to some kind of understanding of what God's will must be in the world today. And this, of course, brings us back to our previous statement that the Incarnation is the central doctrine of the Christian faith today.

A further weakness of the liberalism which we have been describing was an inadequate understanding of the New Testament picture of man. Man in this tradition was thought to be basically good in spite of the mistakes he had made. The doctrine of the basic goodness of mankind was very simply derived. God's creation, according to Genesis, was good. Man is a part of this creation. Therefore man is good. He has made many mistakes, he has opposed his will to that of God, and he has turned away from God. But he has the potential for recovering from these mistakes and returning to God. And given enough time he will do so.

We have discussed previously the philosophy of Hegel and others which led to the notion that progress was inevitable. On the basis of this philosophical position it was thought that the eventual salvation of man was assured. If all the means at his disposal were used to the very best of his ability, man would certainly be able to work out his own salvation. And on the basis of Hegel's work this thesis could be proved to the satisfaction of even the most skeptical. But there was one slight flaw in this whole beautiful theoretical system: It didn't work! The theologians who had convinced themselves of the goodness of man and the inevitability of his building a heaven on earth watched with amazement as World War I proved all of their words false. As even the most civilized of men in Europe turned into brutal killers, the theories of philosophers and theologians crumbled into dust.

As a result of World War I the theology which arose in Europe after 1918 began to take a radically different view of the nature of man. It became necessary to turn back to the writings of Paul in order to find an adequate doctrine of man. Paul's view was that man was created good, but that he had fallen into a condition of sin from which he could never rescue himself. Therefore his only hope of redemption lay with God. And only God could do for man what he was not able to do for himself. We shall deal with the importance of the Pauline view of man for present-day theology in the next chapter.

The death of liberal theology in Europe did not have any immediate effect on theology in the United States. For the people of this country were not as thoroughly involved in World War I as those in Europe. In a sense World War II did for our own theologians what World War I did for those in Germany. The new European theology which had replaced liberalism on the continent began to gather momentum in the United States in the 1940's. In the United States, as in Europe, liberalism had failed to provide a valid *theological* basis for social action in an age which has a desperate need for it.

But if the theological weaknesses of liberalism have rendered it inadequate as a basis for social concern, the theological weaknesses of the fundamentalist reaction have rendered it equally useless for the same purpose. It was true that liberalism had given too much away in its attempt to adapt to modern life. And on the surface fundamentalism was an attempt to conserve that which was vital in the Christian faith, which liberalism had lost. But in a deeper sense fundamentalism was not true conservatism at all. The fundamentalist went beyond conservatism to become reactionary. Conservatism might be defined as hanging on to that which is vital and not allowing social or theological change to take it away. But "reaction," on the other hand, is a desire to recapture the past. It is actually a running away from the present-day situation in an impossible quest to recapture something which can never return. Fundamentalism failed to provide a complete answer to the problem of Christian living, because it refused to take seriously the role of the Christian church in the twentieth century. And the lack of social concern which characterized fundamentalism was a function of this refusal.

In contrast with the worst of liberalism, the theology of fundamentalism had a number of features which seemed to recommend it very highly. In the first place the doctrine of the Incarnation was taken seriously. The Incarnation was seen as a doctrine which expressed God's concern for men and his involvement with them. But this involvement was seen as primarily, if not entirely, a personal involvement with individual men. From the fundamentalist point of view John 3:16 wrapped up the doctrine of the Incarnation. The purpose of God's involvement in human life was that individual men might not perish ultimately but might have eternal life. Valuable as this doctrine was, it did not tell the whole story. For the Incarnation indicates the involvement of God not only with individual men but with the world as a whole. Furthermore the fundamentalist's treatment of Jesus Christ tended to undercut the full meaning of the Incarnation by ignoring his *human* nature.

In the second place fundamentalism did take seriously the doctrines of Sin and Grace. Man was seen in a realistic perspective, as having serious shortcomings about which he could do nothing by himself. It was recognized that salvation depended upon the free grace of God, which man could not buy or win. The only route to salvation, as the author of Ephesians concisely stated, is by the grace of God through faith. (Eph. 2:8.)

On the other hand the salvation which comes by the grace of God through faith in Christ was separated by the fundamentalists from the rest of life. This is not to say that they viewed salvation as having no effect upon the life of a man. But they did feel that for the man who had been "saved," the world no longer made a great deal of difference. The man who was "born again" through the grace of God was a man who had risen above the world and had his reward waiting for him in an eternity which would be spent with God, in another life. The emphasis was not upon the relationship of man to this world but upon rewards in the life to come. Therefore the problems and tribulations of this world were not a primary concern of the Christian. He could put up with almost anything in this life,

87

knowing that the persecution and hardship would not last long, and that his persecution and trouble here would win for him a reward in heaven. Thus religion did not come to terms with the problems of the social order but ignored them and directed the attention of Christians away from them. In this sense this particular brand of religion became the "opiate of the people."

This last phrase should have a familiar and slightly sinister ring to it. For the man who made the accusation popular was Karl Marx, the philosophical father of modern Communism. But can we trust the judgment of the man who dreamed up the worldwide menace which Communism has become?

The hard and unpleasant fact is that Marx was quite correct in his evaluation of the church *of his own day*. He was very much concerned with the problems of poverty, disease, oppression, and ignorance—approximately the same list of problems which concerned the originators of the social gospel movement. But he saw that the church of his day was not concerned with social action in any way. Religion was being used, in his culture, as a means of keeping the lower classes contented so that they would not revolt. Peasants and factory workers were promised that they would have a reward in heaven, and therefore they should not be concerned about unbearable conditions in this life. Therefore Marx turned away from the Christian church and formulated his answer to the problems of society in terms of an atheistic system of social action.

Communism is predicated upon a belief that the church will take no initiative in removing the problems of society. And one of the most effective ways of combating world Communism is for the church to develop and maintain a social conscience and a program of social action, which will make it unnecessary for men to turn to Communism for the relief which they so deseperately seek.[56]

In summary, then, fundamentalism did do a service to Christian theology by taking seriously once again the doctrine of the Incarnation, the doctrine of Sin, and the doctrine of Grace. Unfortunately the implications of these doctrines were not carried as far as they should have been. But there are several points at which the doctrines of fundamentalism were totally inadequate. One of these was the doctrine of Creation.

The world was seen by fundamentalists as being basically evil. It was controlled by Satan, often called "the prince of this world," who constantly attempts to win men away from their loyalty to God. At this point, it seems that the view of Paul concerning creation had been lost or at least badly misinterpreted. Paul's attitude was that the world is good. As a part of God's creation it could not be anything else. However, the world becomes demonic when man allows it to *control* him. Man had allowed the world to come between him and God, and this was wrong.

89

The world, however, was basically good and had been made, according to the purpose of God, to serve man and to be controlled by him. In other words, man was not to avoid the world nor to ignore the world, but simply to see that the things of the world were used for the purposes for which God had created them.

A second doctrine badly misunderstood by fundamentalism was the doctrine of Revelation through Scripture. The Bible was seen as the Word of God. On the other hand there was an insufficient understanding of the role which men played in the development of the Bible. The Bible is, indeed, the Word of God. But it is God's work *through the agency of man.* Fundamentalism in general did not understand the value of critical analysis in discovering what God's Word really is. The fundamentalist tried to pretend that liberalism and biblical criticism had never happened. But a great deal *had* happened which could not be undone. Now any realistic understanding of the Bible had to take seriously the work of literary analysis, history, and the realities of modern science. The attempt to pretend otherwise was futile. It made no more sense than the man who flipped a coin into a wishing-well in the lobby of a theater, saying, "I wish I had not seen that movie!"

In some cases the fundamentalist position on the Bible actually interfered with the effective proclamation of the biblical message. One example of this is the intense opposition which arose in fundamentalist circles to the use of the Revised Standard Version of the Bible. Not only is the Revised Standard Version (and for that matter The New English Bible) translated into modern English, which is much more easily understood by the younger generation, especially, but it is based upon a much more accurate Greek New Testament text than that from which the King James Version was translated.[57] And yet there has been a great deal of opposition to the use of any modern translation in church school literature, simply because it represents a change.[58] Obviously the kind of analysis and sifting described in chaps. 1 and 2 is incompatible with the position which we are describing here. It seems to me that fundamentalism did a disservice to the Christian faith by ruling out some of the processes by which the Word of God can be made to speak more clearly and forcefully to our situation today. Certainly God does not intend his Word to be obscure or difficult, and anything which clarifies its meaning and helps men to apply it to their own situations should be welcomed.

We see, then, that liberalism did have a sense of the social responsibility of the church but was hindered by an inadequate Christology and an inadequate understanding of the nature of man. Furthermore it had very little interest in evangelism of any sort. Fundamentalism, on the other hand, took seriously the Incarnation, the nature of sin, and the necessity for the grace of God. But it held a doctrine of Creation which separated man from the world, and had an inadequate doctrine of Revelation in terms of the nature and significance of the Bible. Therefore fundamentalism had very little effect in making the biblical witness relevant to the problems of mankind.

Since both of these theological extremes had proved to be inadequate, it is necessary for the church today to have a theology which has the strength of both of these positions and the weaknesses of neither. That is to say that today we must have a theology which takes seriously the doctrine of the Incarnation, with its reference to God's personal involvement in history; which has an adequate doctrine of Man, recognizing sin, human nature, and redemption; which has an adequate doctrine of Creation, seeing the world in its proper perspective; and which has a doctrine of Revelation which makes it possible for the Bible to speak clearly to the present generation. In the next chapter we shall try to outline what such a theology may have to say to the church today in terms of the responsibility of the church to the whole man. And this responsibility must include the evangelistic zeal which was so important to fundamentalism, together with some of its orthodoxy, and the social responsibility which characterized liberalism.

7

The Whole Gospel for
the Whole Man

We have seen that the question, "What would Jesus have done in this situation?" is no longer an adequate question in terms of applying the New Testament message to the needs of our society. But if this question is inadequate, what more basic question *should* we ask of the Bible? Simply this: What does the *Act of God in Christ* say to us, as we act today? We can no longer use the Bible as a step by step blueprint for our actions. But it does give us the theological basis for the commitment upon which our actions must be based.

This theological framework for commitment rests upon three doctrines central to the Christian gospel: Incarnation, divine Grace, and divine Love. Let us examine the meaning and demands of each.

The doctrine of Incarnation says that God entered personally and completely into human history. He involved himself directly and fully in the problems and limitations of mankind. Theologians have debated for twenty centuries the proper interpretation of this doctrine and the precise meaning of the statement, "Jesus Christ is God." Some of the most important general councils of the church have been held to deal with the fine points of this issue. These discussions and debates are of extreme importance, but we cannot take time here to sort out the issues involved. Whatever interpretation is placed on the Incarnation, it means that God became personally involved with mankind.

If God saw fit to involve himself in the problems of human society through his act in Jesus Christ, the church as the body of Christ can hardly afford to do less. It is natural for the church to show some reluctance to get involved in such things as crime, vice, politics, poverty, and race riots. But the Incarnation gives us a challenge which we cannot avoid.

Some years ago, at a conference for pretheological students, I heard a young man voice one of the great fears facing the church at this point. "The church," he said, "is a holy institution. If she involves herself in the problems of social action, she may become infected by what she touches. She may be led to compromise her principles in a direct encounter with evil. Isn't it better for her to keep her distance from the quicksand of social problems and simply provide an example of shining virtue, as a goal for society as a whole to reach?"

The murmurs and nods of approval which ran through the group indicated that this young man had touched an area of real concern. But a professor of theology snapped the group back to reality with a few knife-edged words: "I understand the Incarnation to mean that God got his hands dirty in world history! And if God was willing to become involved in the problems of the world, the church can hardly afford to be more holy than God!" If the church is truly the Body of Christ, she has no choice but to become involved in the problems of humanity, no matter how sordid they may be.

The second doctrine on which our understanding of the church's responsibility is based is divine Grace. Grace implies forgiveness, and forgiveness implies sin. And man has always been ready and willing to supply the latter.

An understanding of the grace of God requires an understanding of what we mean by sin. When we use the word sin we are usually referring to a specific wrong action. We say that someone has committed a sin by lying, stealing, or committing adultery. In the letters of Paul, however, the word sin has a different meaning.

For Paul sin is not an action but a state of being. He understands sin as putting God anywhere other than in first place in your life. Man's primary loyalty and commitment should be to God. If a man himself has taken God's rightful place or given it to anything else, then that man is in a state of sin. He is incapable of living a Christian life, because his loyalties are arranged in the wrong order. He may have a place for God in his life, but this does no good unless that place is *first*. If a man is in a state of sin, i.e., if he does not place God first in his life, then he is unable to avoid doing things which are wrong. And these wrong actions, which we usually call "sins," are more properly called "vices." A vice is something which arises naturally as the result of a state of sin in a man's life.

The only cure for sin is to restore God to his rightful place in man's life. It would seem that once man is aware of the problem, nothing would be simpler than doing this. But of course there is a catch. The problem in most cases is that man himself has taken the place which belongs to God. This means that what man has to do is to get himself out of first place in his life and put God back where he belongs. But this means that man is concentrating on *himself* as the main problem in his life and therefore is not able to forget himself and turn to God. This makes it impossible for man to work out his own salvation.

The situation in which man finds himself at this point brings to mind a foolproof formula which was worked out some time ago for turning dirty dishwater into solid gold. The formula is very simple, and it is guaranteed to work if it is carried out according to instructions. All that you have to do is to take a large pan full of dirty dishwater and stir it briskly for some time with a wooden stick. If you stir long enough, the water will turn into solid gold, provided—and this is the most important part—that *never once while you are stirring the dirty*

96

dishwater do you think of a hippopotamus! If you ever think of a hippopotamus while doing the stirring, the entire spell is broken and you will never have the gold. Now just go out and try it! Never again, after having read these words, will you be able to stir dirty dishwater with a wooden stick without thinking of a hippopotamus! Any time that you try it, you will be concentrating so hard on trying NOT to think of a hippopotamus, that you won't be able to think of anything else.[59]

The same problem arises when we try to save ourselves by putting God in first place in our lives. We are concentrating so hard on trying to forget ourselves that self is the only thing we can think about. We put ourselves into the position of a man who is sinking into a bed of quicksand. Any motion that he makes in trying to free himself simply drives him deeper into the quicksand. Because he has no way of getting leverage for an escape, it is completely impossible for him to avoid destruction unless he has outside help. The only thing that he can do is to accept the aid of an outside force with sufficient power to pull him out.

It is in the light of this situation that we see the doctrine of divine Grace. Man is in a very serious situation which goes beyond his individual acts, which traps him in a bed of quicksand from which he cannot rescue himself. But the situation is not hopeless. For God has acted on behalf of man, to do for man that which he cannot do for himself. In

Jesus Christ God has acted in such a way that man's salvation is now possible.

Because we believe in the grace of God, we believe that no human life or social situation is beyond redemption. No matter how far a man may have strayed from God, no matter how bad a social situation may be, the grace of God can heal and redeem, if we will only allow him to work in the situation.

What does this mean, then, in terms of our responsibility as Christians? Does it mean that we should sit back and wait for the grace of God to act, since there is nothing that we can do about the situation ourselves? No! We have two responsibilities, as a church and as individuals. In the first place we must speak clearly and forcefully the word which the gospel has for the situation in question. In the second place we must become involved in the situation in the same way in which God involved himself in human affairs. That is to say, we must offer ourselves as channels of God's grace. We must make ourselves available for him to use us in whatever way he sees fit, that the situation may be redeemed through his grace and love.

The Christian church has always insisted that God is love. That is to say, we know what love is *only* as we confront the actions of God on behalf of man. Among the most familiar words of Jesus in the New Testament are these: "This is my commandment, that you love one another as I have loved you" (John 15:12). The author of I John insists

98

that a man's love for God can be measured by the way in which he acts toward his fellow men. He says that no man can say he loves God if he hates his fellow man. (I John 4:13-21.)

Christian love has been defined by Paul in the immortal words of I Corinthians 13. We might sum up the biblical definition of Christian love by saying that it is "concerned involvement." Concern is an important part of love, but it is not the whole story. Unless my concern for another leads me to become involved in his problems even to the point of sacrificing my own interests to help him, my concern is not real love.

Several years ago I was pastor of a church in a depressed area of metropolitan New Jersey. The neighborhood in which we lived abounded with children of all ages, religions, and races. The area around the church was the place where they always gathered. When I left the house in the morning, there was a large group of children playing on the sidewalks and in the gutters. When I returned home at noon, and again in the evening, the children were still there. When I went to bed, a large group of children could always be seen playing under the streetlights. When a siren or the telephone woke me at three or four o'clock in the morning, the children were still there, playing in the street.

Somewhere in the tenements and bars of the neighborhood, those children had parents. On several occasions, when the children got into trouble, I hunted the parents down to talk with them. Invariably they insisted that they loved their children very much. But their statements of love did not convince me at all. No matter how loudly they said "we love our son," their total lack of concerned involvement in his life showed that they were lying or fooling themselves.

If we say that we love our fellowmen as God has loved us but have no concern for an involvement in problems of society, we are only fooling ourselves. In the last chapter of John the risen Christ asked Peter three times, "Do you love me?" Three times Peter replies, "Yes, Lord; you know that I love you!" The passage ends with a challenge to Peter: "If you love me, feed my sheep!" Feeding the sheep of Christ was to be the witness of Peter to the love which he said he had for Christ himself. And our love for Christ is tested in the same way. If we fail to feed his sheep, then our words concerning love for God and love for man are hollow mockeries.

Feeding the sheep of Christ means more than just preaching the Christian gospel to them. It is not enough to stand up and proclaim the Word of God. The prophets in the Old Testament did that much, and it was not enough. It was necessary for God to become totally involved in the problems of the world, in person. If speaking the Word of God to society was not enough in the time of the prophets, it is not enough today. The church as the Body of Christ, i.e., the extension of the incarnation, must

100

have a concern for the problems of the world and become involved in doing something about them. And this involvement must take the form of an acceptance and love of persons, and an involvement in social change.

An acceptance and love of persons is not to be underestimated in its importance. A simple proclamation of the realities of the Christian gospel may do nothing more than shatter the life of the person who hears the message. A case in point is the apostle Paul, who was confronted by the risen Christ on the road to Damascus. In his conversion experience Paul was presented with the challenge of the Christian gospel. In a flash everything which had been important to him previously was turned into dust and ashes. When the experience was over, he arose from his knees a blinded and broken man. With the help of his friends he managed to stagger on into the city of Damascus and to find refuge in a dark room in the house of a friend. For some time he lay there in the room, tossing about in pain and in confusion.

Everything which had been important to Paul was now meaningless. He had been a Pharisee, a defender of the law. Now he saw that the law of God, as found in the books of Moses, could not bring about man's salvation. He had been an orthodox Jew. Now the principles of Judaism, which had been so meaningful, had no comfort and support for him. He had been a persecutor of the Christians and had felt

101

a great sense of pride in helping to wipe out this menace to his faith. Now he saw that he had been going in the wrong direction in his opposition to the church. He had been a man of high position in Jerusalem with many powerful and influential friends. Now that he had renounced Judaism they turned their backs on him in contempt. Everything upon which Paul had leaned and depended for strength was now snatched away from him, and he was without hope. He knew that Christ had claimed his life, but he had no idea what that meant in terms of the days ahead.

And then into Paul's dark room there walked a man named Ananias. Ananias did not believe that Paul was really a convert. He feared very strongly that this was just a trick which Paul was using to find out the identity of the Christians in Damascus. He had no more faith in Paul than we would have if ex-Premier Khrushchev should arrive in this country by jet, state that he had renounced Communism, and ask to be made a part of our government so that he could help fight international Communism.

All the Christians in Damascus regarded Paul's conversion as a new variation of the Trojan horse trick. But Ananias was a man of faith. He had been asked in a vision to go to Paul and receive him into the Christian faith as a brother. When Ananias stretched out his hand to touch Paul and called him "brother," Paul suddenly understood the meaning of Christian love. He knew the fear which was in

102

the heart of this man as he came into the presence of one who had been a murderer of his fellow-Christians. He saw that this man in spite of his fear was willing, because of Christian love, to accept him as a brother in Christ. At that moment the scales fell from the eyes of Paul and he was able to see. From that moment on he was a new man in Christ. The acceptance and love which he experienced at the hands of Ananias made it possible for him to understand the real meaning of Christian love and Christian fellowship. He rose from his bed to go forth to preach the gospel of Christ to a dark world.

Our love for, and acceptance of, those who have heard the proclamation and challenge of Christ is a most important part of evangelism. We go forth with great enthusiasm to preach the gospel of Christ and to present his challenge to a world which does not know him. It is well that we do so! But what happens to the people who are touched by our proclamation, and who present themselves at the altar of the church for membership? Do they receive the kind of love and personal concern which are needed if they are to become a part of the fellowship of Christ's church? Are we concerned enough for them as persons to involve ourselves in their problems and to give them the support which they need as they take their first faltering steps as followers of Christ? We must not forget that in presenting the claims of Christ upon them we have wiped out everything which was previously important to them. Those things which formerly gave them support and guidance are now meaningless. We must make sure that something is provided to take their place. But when we are most needed to uphold and sustain those whom we have challenged to follow Christ, we are too often out on other business and unable to give the help which is needed.

Not only must we be concerned about the persons whom we confront with the Christian gospel, but we must also be involved in changing the society which grinds men into the dirt of crime and depravity. This is where evangelism and social concern join hands. There are some problems in our society which simply cannot be solved by dealing with individuals. In order to come to terms with these problems, we must come to grips with the causes of the social diseases behind them. The Christian church must be vitally concerned today with problems of automation, narcotics, peace and world order, and human rights and dignity. We must make ourselves channels for the grace of God, not only in terms of proclaiming his witness to individuals, but in terms of redeeming the society of which individuals are a part.

Let me illustrate my point in terms of a case which recently came to my attention. A minister was told that a brutal father in his parish was systematically abusing his teen-age child. Investigation on the part of the minister proved that these charges were well founded. The situation was a very unfortunate one. The pastor took the case to the juvenile authorities of the community, who immediately moved to protect the child. At the same time the pastor provided continual guidance and spiritual support. Within a very short time the child had been taken out of the home. The father was locked up to be held for trial. The child was locked up in the children's detention home, which was actually a wing of the county jail! The trial of the father was scheduled for several weeks later. Within twenty-four hours the father was out on bail. The child remained in the detention home. No foster home could be found, because no one wanted to take in a fifteen-year-old child. The pastor and his wife offered to take the child in, but this was against the rules of the juvenile authorities. It was feared that an emotional attachment might develop, which would cause trouble when the child was moved. While the pastor and authorities worried about the situation, the child sat in prison for several weeks.

Obviously there is something wrong with a system which allows a father like this to go free immediately, while the innocent party who is being "protected" by law sits in jail. One of the functions of the church in this case is to provide Christian love and support for the child and to present the claims of Christ to this father, in the hope that he might change his ways. But the responsibility does not end here. It is also the task of the church to become involved in this social situation and to help bring about a change in the laws and practices of this community, so that such a case of injustice will not happen again. An investigation of the situation in the home may well open up two or three other areas of concern in which action by the church is indicated.

We can see, then, that the responsibility of the church rests upon the three doctrines of Incarnation, Grace, and Love. The doctrine of Incarnation tells us that we must become involved in the problems of mankind. The doctrine of Grace tells us that the situation is very serious, but that it is not hopeless if we will make ourselves available as channels of grace. The doctrine of Love tells us that we must have a concerned involvement which goes beyond a simple proclamation of our belief to those outside the fold. We must deal with the problems of persons and go beyond these to change the social situations which are making their lives intolerable.

Oddly enough, the Christian church usually sees its evangelistic task in the proper light in the mission field, but not at home. Mission boards no longer send only preachers to Africa and Asia, as they once did. They take responsibility for the total welfare of the people they serve. Therefore they send and support doctors, dentists, teachers, nurses, agriculturalists, *and* ministers. All of them work together to minister to the spiritual and physical needs of the people while working toward creative changes in their environment. Yet many people who give strong support to this policy on the foreign mission field have failed to see that *both* personal evangelism and social action are vital parts of the church's total witness in our *own* society.

8

Where Do We Begin?

It may sound strange to call the final chapter of a book, "Where do we begin?" But all that we have covered so far is simply *background* for responsible Christian social action. We have looked at the problems of interpreting biblical material in today's world and at the ways in which the church has applied the Bible to social problems in the past. It now becomes our job to apply the biblical message to the problems of the world as we see them today, as we minister to the needs of society.

Scope

The task is not an easy one. As we try to make the Christian faith relevant to the needs of the world, there are a number of questions to be asked and guidelines to be established. One of the first questions which must be faced is the proper *scope* of Christian social action. How far can the church go in speaking to social issues? Are there areas of political, economic, and social concern in which the church should remain silent and leave matters wholly in the hands of professionals?

It is easy to see that the church has a responsibility to speak out on such matters as liquor control and the sale of pornography. But the picture is not so clear when it comes to the United Nations, the War on Poverty, or the John Birch Society. Many people feel that such issues as world peace, labor disputes, school integration, and the public debt are beyond the responsibility of the church. They quote Jesus' injunction to "render to Caesar the things that are Caesar's and to God the things that are God's." This they take to mean that political responsibility and religious responsibility are quite separate and should be kept that way.

Jesus' statement has to be understood in its context. He was replying to a trick question which was intended to trip him up. It was shortly after Palm Sunday, and he was in the Jerusalem temple. Crowds of Jews surrounded him, and the Roman guards watched every movement and listened to every word spoken. Their presence in the temple was a source of resentment in the hearts of the Jews. They were a constant reminder of the force of the hated foreign rulers, controlling every aspect of life. As both Jews and Romans listened intently, someone asked Jesus a question: "Is it lawful [for a God-fearing Jew] to pay taxes to Caesar?"

The crowd pressed closer as Jesus wrinkled his brow in thought. If he said that taxes required by Caesar were to be ignored, the soldiers would arrest him for preaching treason in public. If he said that taxes *should* be paid to Caesar, he might be attacked by militant Jews who bitterly opposed any recognition of Roman power. It seemed to be a trap with no way out!

But Jesus took a coin and noted that it had Caesar's picture on it and therefore could be given to Caesar in taxes. Caesar and God should each be given that which belonged to him. Both groups had to settle for this, and the crisis passed.

But what did Jesus actually say? He insisted that a religious man had a responsibility to serve God and give him his due. But he also said that this religious man had a responsibility to fulfill his obligations as a citizen. His loyalty to God did not remove his responsibility to political authorities. And it is hard to imagine that Jesus meant that a man's religious orientation and loyalty should be separated from his actions as a citizen. He taught that everything a man did should be centered around his commitment to God.

In spite of this witness to the Christian's political responsibility, there are many people who feel in all sincerity that political action is improper for the church. They argue that the church should spend its time studying and teaching the Bible. In this way it will be possible to change individual men's lives and bring about a better world. But the Bible itself is full of stories about political power struggles, wars, and economic crises. And many of the leading biblical characters were totally involved in these

110

affairs. Any realistic study and use of the Bible will lead us into social and political issues.

This brings us back to our original question: What issues and problems lie within the social concern of the church? The answer would seem to be: All of them!

Methods

If all areas of political, social, and economic concern are open to the Christian church as areas where a witness is required, the next question must be: What methods and procedures are appropriate for this witness? To begin with, one of the most important roles which the church can play in social action is that of educator.

No one can function intelligently as a Christian citizen unless he has enough information at his disposal. He needs an understanding of the biblical message and the faith of the Christian church. He also needs to know the facts concerning the issues facing our legislators and administrators. Beyond this he needs a working knowledge of the machinery of government.

The church should be educating its membership in all these areas. Through pulpit and church school there should be a program of continuing education for adults in the Bible and Christian doctrine. Many adults take Christian education very lightly except for their children, but it is essential for adults. If

111

refresher courses are necessary periodically in business and the professions, they are no less important in the church.

A social action committee of the local church might provide opportunities for studying the current political and economic crises. All sides of today's crucial issues should be explored, so that churchmen may make intelligent decisions based on the facts. In order to implement these decisions it is necessary to know where lines of responsibility lie in terms of federal, state, and local government. Some time ago a group of laymen who serve in positions of political responsibility gave their reactions to the question of responsible Christian citizenship, in *Together* magazine. One of the points made by Senator Tower of Texas was that many people try to make their opinions known without knowing how to do so effectively. Letters are sent to U.S. senators and congressmen concerning state issues. Governors and state legislators are asked to do something about federal tax cases. A great deal of energy is wasted when proper channels of authority and influence are ignored. The church can perform an important educational task at this point.

But education by itself is not enough. In order to be effective an education program must produce action. What sort of action? What can churches and churchmen do to practice what they preach?

The most obvious type of social action available to individuals and groups is letter-writing. A few concerned laymen with typewriters or pens can exert a great deal of influence over important decisions. Most people think government officials get so many letters that one or a dozen more or less won't make any difference. Not so! One rather highly placed official told me a few years ago that receipt of fifty or more letters opposing his department's policy on a given issue always caused them to reopen the issue and reexamine their position.

To be effective the letters have to meet certain tests. Each letter should deal with only one issue. It should show that the writer has considered all sides of the issue and come to an intelligent decision. All government offices are flooded with crank letters from people who think with their viscera, not their minds. These have no effect. Neither do mimeographed letters or form letters composed by a pressure group and dutifully copied off by members. Never send more than one letter at a time, either. Some groups, such as the John Birch Society, have urged members to send six or more letters, each signed with a different name. This practice is not only ethically questionable, but it hurts the cause which it is intended to help when the deception is discovered.

If you take your letter-writing seriously, you will find that local, state, and federal law makers and officials will appreciate your concern and sense of responsibility. More often than not this appreciation will be expressed in an answering letter. Once you have written to a legislator—let's say your congressman—watch the newspaper to see how he votes on various issues. When you feel that he has voted wisely, tell him so. Even politicians like to know that they are appreciated.

Although letter-writing is important, it is only one of several ways in which you can make your opinions known. Sometimes it helps to get a group together locally to air current social problems and try to work out solutions. The church is an excellent place for public debate on public issues in a climate of Christian concern and fair play. Usually the local commission on Christian social concerns can find within the church informed members who can speak on both sides of a given controversial issue. Sometimes it is wise to go outside the church and invite guest experts in to voice their views and to respond to questions in an open forum. Not only is a church forum on current events a good way to keep the congregation informed, but it may serve to arouse the interest of the whole community in the church. A well-planned debate on an issue of current importance is worthy of at least a column of newspaper space, especially if an outside expert is to speak. And when the public sees that the church is involved in the crucial issues of the day, a new interest may be aroused in many who have long considered the church irrelevant and self-centered.

On occasion social concern must take people outside the walls of the church into the marketplace. When there is a Christian witness to be made and

114

the crowd ignores the church, the church must speak directly to the crowd. But how can you get the attention of people who are wrapped up in their own concerns? Sometimes it is necessary to use some sort of shock treatment to wake them up.

The problem is not a new one. Several of the Old Testament prophets had messages of great importance for the people and the rulers of their nations, which no one wanted to hear. Jeremiah, for example, talked himself hoarse on the subject of Judah's relationship with Babylon, and no one heard him. Finally he appeared in public one day with an ox yoke on his shoulders. As he walked up and down the street, crowds of curious people gathered to see the fun. When he had their attention, Jeremiah explained that the yoke was a symbol of God's judgment upon the people of Judah for their sins.

Isaiah once noticed that the people who paid no attention to his preaching would stand for hours listening to love songs sung by troubadours with lutes. So Isaiah wrote a love song, found a lute, and went into the street as a troubadour. But his love song had a sharply pointed message: if Judah did not return to God, she would be destroyed. (Isa. 5.)

What was appropriate for the prophets is still appropriate today. There are times when groups of Christians must go out into the streets and dramatize their message so that no one can ignore it. This may involve a public rally. It may mean a march on a state capitol building. It may mean carrying a placard.

Public demonstration of this sort is not a lark. It is not to be engaged in without the most careful and prayerful deliberation. But there are times when it must be done.

During a recent election campaign one local political organization began distributing a slanderous attack on several Protestant churches, as campaign literature. Efforts to reason with the responsible officials met with no success. Finally a large group of ministers held a demonstration at the organizational headquarters. The purpose was to call public attention to the fact that there were two sides to the issue and to get wide circulation for a pamphlet which answered the lies in the campaign literature. Some people were shocked to see clergymen in a picket line and accused the ministers of "stooping to the tactics of labor unions and Negroes." Had they been more familiar with the Old Testament prophets, they would have known that the nonviolent demonstrations of minority groups in recent years have a biblical origin. From the standpoint of Christian ethics any sort of orderly, legal demonstration is justified if its purpose is to call the attention of the public to a legitimate Christian concern.

Of course there are situations where letter-writing, debating, and demonstrating are not enough. If persuasion aimed at those in authority fails and you feel that a new hand is needed at the helm, your Christian concern may lead you directly into a political campaign. It is always difficult to get leaders of the church—lay or clergy—to run for office or to work on a campaign. They are apt to feel that politics is a dirty business and that a Christian should stay away from it. But to do so is to place politics in the hands of the unethical and unscrupulous. There is a time for a Christian to be a candidate or support a candidate as a vital part of his service to God and country.

Depth

If, as we have suggested, the church should be involved in *all* social issues and has *all* legal and ethical methods and resources at her disposal, we must now ask the question, "How deeply should the church be involved in society and its problems?" The answer would seem to depend on circumstances.

Through its individual laymen the church can and should be involved at the most basic level in political and social affairs. Christian laymen should seek and serve in both elective and appointive political offices. They should have a knowledge of the Bible and of Christian doctrine, which can inform their decisions concerning the public interest. They should take advantage of lay theology courses and make use of the pastors and theologians of their churches, as resources in their work. Too often a legislator or administrator prides himself on his church relationship, but it has no effect on his decisions. His relationship to the church consists only of

117

occasional-to-regular attendance at morning worship services. His knowledge of theology and the Bible are limited to what he learned in Sunday school, as a child. He has little or no conception of the moral and theological dimensions of many political and social issues. In fact, the major political value of his church relationship lies in the area of public relations. This is a political pattern which should be broken by dedicated and theologically sensitive Christian laymen who are willing to involve themselves in the "dirty business" of politics.

So the church *can* be involved in politics through its laymen. But what about its ministers? Can they afford to be involved? Certainly they have a concern for the good of society and a responsibility to speak out on moral issues. But what if the "good of society" and the "moral issues" come down to a partisan political battle? What if the minister's involvement in a problem will put him in direct opposition to the opinions or the efforts of parishioners?

A number of arguments have been used to persuade ministers to stay out of political and economic affairs. One of the favorites is to remind the pastor of his responsibility to his people. "Pastor, your job is to preach on Sunday, run the church, and talk with people who come to you for help. You should stay out of politics and do the job you are paid for!" Obviously the thesis of this book is that political and economic affairs cannot be separated from the mission of the church as a whole. Therefore the pastor

118

is not "stepping outside his role" when he gets involved in a civil rights drive or a campaign to end capital punishment. In dealing with people and issues in the very sewers of society, the minister is following in the footsteps of his Lord. On Holy Thursday, 1965, the editorial cartoonist of the *Kansas City Star* made this point in the drawing reproduced in the front of this book.

Another argument often heard is that ministers must protect their positions as authorities on matters of faith and morals. If a minister takes sides on a partisan political issue and uses his position in the church to express his opinion, those on the other side of the political fence will lose their confidence in him, and he will alienate himself from them. How can they respect his pronouncements as a pastor when he is opposing them politically? The argument sounds plausible. But there are many ways for a minister to lose the respect of his congregation. How can churchmen respect a minister who stands in the pulpit week after week, telling them to live their faith, and then does not leave his own study to meet the problems facing society? A man who does not have the courage of his convictions can hardly lead people toward the kingdom of God.

But the minister should never forget his position nor compromise it. He can never allow himself the luxury of the politician's "my party, right or wrong!" He must always remember that his service is to the Lord and not to a particular political or economic theory to which he may be attracted for its own sake.

There comes a time, of course, when the involvement of the church in social issues goes beyond individual action—either clergy or lay—to group action. Such action usually involves a group *within* the church rather than the congregation as a whole, since unanimity of opinion on controversial issues is rare, and Protestant churches are supposed to be democratic organizations.

Groups within the church have the same opportunities and responsibilities in regard to action projects as individuals.

We have argued that the church must be involved in the world if she is to fulfill her mission. However, she cannot sacrifice her complete devotion to Christ and his kingdom in the process. Christian social action is a complex and demanding responsibility. It is not easy to apply one's Christian faith to the complicated and knotty problems facing our nation today. There is a constant need for reevaluation and rethinking of one's position. The Christian who commits himself to one course of action, in good conscience, after weighing all of the evidence sometimes finds that his position has side effects which he would rather avoid. So a Christian political witness is usually as difficult as it is necessary.

Some people want to make this very uncomfortable process an easy, painless task. The only way to do this is to oversimplify your responsibility. Pick out only one idea as being of any importance—"less government control," for example, or "ban the bomb," or "hate Communists." Then concentrate all your energy and commitment on that one idea. Convince yourself that the whole Christian gospel is wrapped up in it alone.

Look at everything in terms of stark blacks and whites instead of admitting that there are shades of gray. Or pick an organization which is generally in agreement with your beliefs and sanctify it. Convince yourself that it can do no wrong. Equate its ideas with *the* Christian faith. Then you can serve your one idea or one group and never be uncomfortable. You never need to do any painful soul searching or theological thinking.

There is one small problem with this plan, however. It forces you to commit idolatry. When you make *any* single idea or *any* group the equal of your faith in God, you become an idolater. The reason that men of old made idols of wood and metal was that it made service to God easier. They could not see God and therefore did not know quite how to worship him. They made images of familiar objects, which they knew were God's creations, and tried to worship him through them. And thus they violated the First Commandment.

A Christian must, by definition, be an extremist in his faith and commitment. But if he becomes an extremist in any other sense, he has committed idolatry. No idea or cause may be substituted for God in the Christian's loyalty.

121

One unfortunate element in certain types of political and economic extremism is the belief that evil is irreversible or beyond the redemptive power of God. If evil is irreversible, then the only way to deal with it is to eliminate it. Elimination of the evil means eliminating those who practice it. Since evil is irreversible, *they* are beyond the possibility of redemption. Any contact with them can only result in the contamination of the righteous man by the force of evil. The righteous fanatic scorns those who are "soft" on something known to be evil and waits for the time when sin will not exist, because all the sinners will be eliminated.

The Christian gospel, however, insists that evil is reversible. Evil is not to be ignored, but it is not so powerful as the love of God. The man captured by evil can be won back from it by the power of that love. If men can be redeemed by God's love, so can institutions and nations. Christians are not called to hate and destroy sinners but to serve as channels for God's grace.

The way of Christian service to man and God is not easy—few worthwhile things are. As Christians we know that we have a responsibility to witness to our faith where that witness is most needed. But it is so easy to settle for filling a comfortable pew on Sunday morning.

The church is in danger of becoming like the actor in an old-fashioned vaudeville skit: as the scene opens, the stage is dark except for a single street light which illuminates a ten-foot circle of light. A man enters the circle of light and walks around and around the lamp post with eyes fixed on the ground. A policeman enters and asks the man what he is doing. "Looking for my lost key," is the reply. The policeman joins the search, and both walk around the lamp post for several minutes. Finally, when no key is found, the policeman straightens up and stops the man. "Are you sure you lost your key here?" "No, I lost it two blocks down the street." "Then why aren't you looking for it there?" "Because the light is so much better here!"

If the church is to bring the gospel to those who need it most, it will have to venture out of its comfortable circle of light into the darkness of the world. That is where evangelism must be carried on, because that is where people are lost.

But while we are seeking for people in the darkness, we must also try to do something to dispel the darkness itself. In other words, we must try to change the world even as we carry on evangelism. Is it worth the effort? The darkness is so vast, and we are so weak and helpless.

As Christians we don't really have a choice! If we have the light, we must share it and spread it. For, in the words of the apostle John, Christ is the light which shines in the darkness; and the darkness has not been able to quench that light. And in the words of Christ himself, "*You* are the light of the world!"

Notes

1

1. The Greek Old Testament, or Septuagint (abbr: LXX), was a product of Hellenistic Judaism in the 3rd century B.C. The O.T. quotations in the N.T. are not identical with the Septuagint version which we have today, in many cases, but are quite close to it. We can assume that most N.T. writers were familiar with the Greek Old Testament rather than the original Hebrew.
2. See, e.g., S. Sandmel, *The Hebrew Scriptures* (New York: Knopf, 1963), pp. 190 ff., and S. Blank, *Prophetic Faith in Isaiah* (New York: Harper, 1958), pp. 86 ff. Blank reads the suffering referred to in Isa. 53 as a reference to the Exile and therefore a past event from the author's viewpoint.
3. The importance of the Exodus-Wilderness accounts for Jewish theology can hardly be overestimated. For here we find the beginnings of the doctrine of Election, the basis for the covenant relationship between God and his people, and the tradition of the law-giving on Mt. Sinai.

2

4. See Gen. 4:10-15, and esp. Gen. 9:18-27. Canaan, who is cursed in 9:25 ff., is sometimes falsely represented as the ancestor of the Negro race.
5. See, e.g., Gen. 24:1-4, Deut. 7:1-4. These people were the Canaanites, the "sons of Canaan."
6. E.g., Joel 3:4-8, Obad., Nahum.

7. See Ezra 9:10–10:44.
8. See Judg. 3:1-5, esp. vs. 5.
9. See II Sam. 5.
10. A knowledge of biblical Hebrew is sufficient to read many Phoenician, Moabite, and Canaanite texts.
11. See Amos 9:7.
12. The Philistines seem to have originated on the southern coast of Asia Minor, and the Arameans in Mesopotamia. The origins of the terms "Caphtor" and "Kir" are obscure.
13. See esp. 5:25-27.
14. See Jer. 29:1-8, part of a letter sent by Jeremiah to the exiles in Babylon.
15. See Amos, chaps. 1 and 2.
16. The writings referred to here are those of the priestly (P.) tradition. Any good introduction to the literature of the O.T. will give the background of this tradition and indicate where it can be found in the Pentateuch.
17. See Hab. 1:5–2:3, esp.
18. This is the anonymous prophet whose message is found in the book of Isaiah, chaps. 40–55. For the basis on which this literary division is made, see a good commentary on Isa. 40 ff. (e.g., *The Interpreter's Bible,* [Nashville: Abingdon Press, 1956], V, 381 ff.).
19. Isa. 45:1 ff.
20. Isa. 49:5-6.
21. See J. Pritchard, ed., *Ancient Near Eastern Texts Related to the Old Testament* (Princeton: Princeton U. Press, 1955). Translation of a foundation tablet, pp. 316-17, of Xerxes I (485-465). "Furthermore, there were among those countries (some) which performed (religious) festival to the 'Evil (God) s,' (but) under the 'shadow' of Ahuramazda I eradicated these temples of the 'Evil (God).' "

3

22. The parallel is found in the fact that Mordecai was the one who saved his people from destruction. The publish-

ing house in question is *The Scripture Press.* However, this approach is widely used in nondenominational church school curriculum publications.

23. For an introduction to the allegorical method of biblical interpretation and its dangers, see R. M. Grant, "History of the Interpretation of the Bible," in *The Interpreter's Bible,* I, 106 ff.

24. For an interpretation of the Aldersgate experience, see Luccock and Hutchinson, *The Story of Methodism* (Nashville: Abingdon Press, 1949), pp. 65 ff.

4

25. For a description of Luther's social and economic outlook, see W. Walker, *A History of the Christian Church* (Edinburgh: T & T Clarke, 1949), pp. 352 ff.

26. For a discussion of deism and *laissez faire* economics, see any reliable history of Western civilization or "The Enlightenment." The classic critique of *laissez faire* economics is J. M. Keynes, *The End of Laissez-faire* (London: Hogarth Press, 1927).

27. Even among Presbyterian laymen, there is a significant lack of knowledge of, and faith in, the doctrine of Predestination. The common practice of choosing a church in a nice community on the basis of convenience, rather than doctrine, has brought large numbers of Baptists, Methodists, Disciples, and others into Presbyterian churches by transfer. Too often, in *all* Protestant churches it is assumed that the adult who joins a church by transfer has received adequate instruction in the Christian faith (!) and will somehow or other discover and accept the theology of the church he is joining. The standard presentation of the doctrine of Predestination is in Calvin's *Institutes of the Christian Religion.*

28. For a further discussion of the social consequence of Calvinism see R. H. Tawney, *Religion and the Rise of Capitalism* (New York: Mentor MT 507), chap. ii.

29. For a typical upper-class reaction to Wesley, see the remarks of the Duchess of Buckingham, quoted in Luccock

and Hutchinson, *The Story of Methodism* (Nashville: Abingdon Press, 1949), pp. 99-100.

30. For a biography of Whitefield, see Luccock and Hutchinson, *op. cit.*

31. This provision is still included in the General Rules of The Methodist Church, in the most recent *Discipline*.

32. The leader in the political fight against slavery was William Wilberforce (1759-1833) who died a month before the Emancipation Act was passed but did more than any other single man to bring it about. One of Wesley's last acts before his death was to send a letter of encouragement to the young Wilberforce as he embarked on his lifelong crusade.

33. Wilberforce is a case in point. Other examples would be Robert Raikes who began a system of parochial schools, and John Howard, a prison reform leader.

34. See William E. H. Lecky, *England in the Eighteenth Century,* 8 vols. (London, 1878-90), III, 630 ff.

5

35. For a historian's definition and discussion of historicism, see Hans Meyerhoff, *The Philosophy of History in Our Time* (Garden City, N. Y.: Doubleday [Anchor], 1959), Part I, "The Heritage of Historicism."

36. These written records took the forms of manuscripts, clay tablets, monumental inscriptions, tomb decorations, depending on age and country. Any good history of Near Eastern archaeology will describe the finding of these materials.

37. The fascinating story of the deciphering of the dead languages of the ancient world is told in Johannes Friedrich, *Extinct Languages* (New York: Philosophic Library, 1957).

38. For the story of the development of Near Eastern archaeology, see G. A. Barton, *Archaeology and the Bible* (Philadelphia: Union Press, 1937).

39. Perhaps the most valuable and certainly the most fascinating development in archaeology was the development

of a precise method for dating pieces of pottery on the basis of form, type of clay, and decoration. See W. F. Albright, *The Archaeology of Palestine* (Garden City, N. Y.: Doubleday [Anchor], 1956).

40. This study of oral tradition in the Bible is known as "form criticism" or "form history." For a concise introduction to this discipline see the article "Form Criticism," by K. Grobel, *The Interpreter's Dictionary of the Bible* (Nashville: Abingdon Press, 1962), II, 320-21.

41. James Hutton was the first scientist to seek an answer to the questions of the origin of the world in a study of rocks. His thesis was first presented in 1795 in a paper read to the Royal Society of Edinburgh.

42. See Shailer Mathews, *The Faith of Modernism* (New York: Macmillan, 1924), esp. chap. II.

43. For a biographical sketch, bibliography, and summary of the thought of Hegel, see W. Windelband, *A History of Philosophy*, II, 571 ff. (New York: Harper Torchbook #39).

44. The classical study of all the portraits of the "historical Jesus" is A. Schweitzer, *Von Reimarus zu Wrede,* trans. into English under the title, *The Quest for the Historic Jesus* (New York: Macmillan paperback).

45. The theological position which we have been describing in this chapter answered to either name.

46. A vivid description of the situation to which we refer can be found in the books of Lincoln Steffens and the novels of Frank Norris.

47. The term "social gospel" can be traced to Walter Rauschenbusch, *A Theology of the Social Gospel* (New York: Macmillan, 1917). His Social Gospel philosophy was first set forth in *Christianity and the Social Crisis* (New York: Macmillan, 1907).

48. Mark 12:17 and parallels. This statement can now be seen as a means of avoiding the issue raised by Jesus' antagonists. See p. 109.

49. Acts 4:34-35. This passage is the basis for the famous phrase coined by Karl Marx, "From each, according to his ability. To each, according to his need."

50. In conversation with the author at a minister's meeting in 1954, Thomas noted that all the "important" planks in his original Socialist Party platform had been accepted in principle by both major political parties by 1952.

51. The name can probably be traced to a series of tracts called *The Fundamentals,* published by conservative scholars and theologians, beginning in 1909.

52. For a brief but perceptive summary of the relationship between Protestant scholasticism and fundamentalism, see S. L. Greenslade, *The Cambridge History of the Bible, The West from the Reformation to the Present Day* (New York: Cambridge U. Press, 1963), pp. 306 ff.

53. The social gospel as articulated by Rauschenbusch, and social reform involving political and economic action were largely identified with liberalism. Dr. Timothy Smith in *Revivalism and Social Reform* (Nashville: Abingdon Press, 1957) has made a strong case for the social concern of the American revivalists of the 19th century. His point is well established, with exhaustive documentation. But the social witness of which he speaks differs significantly from that of the social gospelists in several particulars. It emphasizes *personal commitment* as the primary answer to social problems instead of a radical reshaping of social patterns. For example, his chapter on "The Churches Help the Poor" deals primarily with relief of specific instances of poverty rather than all-out attacks on the underlying social and economic causes of poverty.

6

54. Perhaps the best examples of what I have termed "19th-century liberalism" today can be found in the Universalist-Unitarian tradition.

55. See note 44.

56. For further discussion of this point, see C. Bangs, *The Communist Encounter* (Boston: Beacon Hill Press, 1962). This study guide, published by the Church of the Naza-

rene, is an excellent introduction to a study of the relationship between Marxist thought and the Christian faith.

57. The King James Bible was translated in 1611. In 1624, the Patriarch of Constantinople sent a Greek manuscript to King James. When it was examined by English scholars, it was found to be a copy of the Greek Bible from the 5th century A.D. The "Received Text" of the New Testament, then in use in England, on which the KJV had been based, depended on manuscripts at least 700 years later than Alexandrinus (as this new discovery was named), and the 5th-century manuscript was apparently much more accurate. The finding of Alexandrinus touched off a search for other ancient Greek N.T. manuscripts. In the Vatican Library, scholars found a 4th-century A.D. manuscript which had been there for at least two centuries, unnoticed. The finding of a large number of ancient manuscripts of the N.T. opened a new era of N.T. scholarship, in which an attempt was made to reconstruct the original text of the Greek. But none of this information was available to the men who produced the KJV.

58. The charge has been made that the RSV is less orthodox, or more liberal, than the King James Bible. This is not the case. Those who make the charge would do well to compare the two translations of Titus 2:13.

7

59. For this formula, I am indebted to Dr. Lawrence Bash, pastor of the Country Club Christian Church in Kansas City, Missouri.

Questions for Discussion

1. The Dilemma of the Old Testament

1. Where does the Bible get its authority? How did it come to be accepted as the Word of God? Read II Kings 22, the story of the first book to be called "God's Word."
2. Who decided which books to include in the Bible? On what basis? When? A good place to begin finding answers would be the articles on Old Testament and New Testament canon in *The Interpreter's Bible* and *The Interpreter's Dictionary of the Bible*.
3. What does it mean to say that the Bible is "inspired"? Could there be more than one way of defining "inspiration"?
4. Does chapter 1 help to explain why there are different branches of Judaism today, such as "orthodox" and "reform"?

2. Amos or Ezra?

1. How did the religious and political situation of the Hebrews affect their attitudes toward foreigners?
2. Which of these attitudes are most meaningful for us today?
3. What does the Book of Jonah have to say about our

attitude toward other nations, including those behind the Iron and Bamboo curtains?

4. What is the value of a biblical commentary in discovering the meaning of a biblical passage?

3. Christ Is the Yardstick

1. Why does the Christian say that all theology is Christology?

2. How did Paul's experience of the "Christ event" on the road to Damascus change his belief in God? (See Acts 9; I Cor. 15.)

3. How does our belief in Christ as the "center point of history" give a Christian meaning to history?

4. Is your church, in your community, a "posttype" of the Christ event? How?

4. Deists, Calvinists, and Wesley

1. Why did the churches founded by Luther and Calvin have little interest in "social action" in the 18th century? Is this lack of interest still found in Lutheran and Presbyterian churches today? Why?

2. Is "institutionalism" still a problem for the church today? Does it have the same form as in the 18th century? What can be done about it?

3. Is "deism" still a live issue today? If so, where is it found? Is *"laissez faire"* economic theory still a part of our political scene? If so, is it still tied to deism?

4. What economic group made up Wesley's first congregations and "societies"? Is this the same group *now* found in Methodist and other "Wesleyan" churches? Why?

5. Social Action—and Reaction

1. What changes did 19th-century science bring about in Christian theology? Is the same process still going on?
2. Why were "liberalism" and the "social gospel" related so closely?
3. Was fundamentalism an adequate answer to liberalism, in terms of the 20th century? Why?
4. How would you react to the statement that there is no conflict between science and religion, but only between "scientism" and religion, or between science and "religionism"?

6. The Gospel for Today

1. Why is it said that 19th-century liberalism had an "inadequate Christology"? Why is Christology important? Isn't it enough to "believe in God"?
2. How do the different views of man's nature discussed in this chapter compare with the view of Paul in Romans 1 and 2? With the view of Amos?
3. Why did the two World Wars in this century have such a great effect on Protestant theology? Is the "cold war" having any effect on today's theology?
4. Is either liberalism or fundamentalism a live option as a relevant personal theology today? Why?

7. The Whole Gospel for the Whole Man

1. How is the doctrine of God's Incarnation related to social action? Does it tell us *what kind* of action is appropriate?

2. What does it mean for a person or a group to become a channel for God's grace?
3. Do you agree that it is impossible for man to save himself? Why?
4. Is salvation a personal thing or a social process, or both?

8. Where Do We Begin?

1. What is the meaning for us, today, of Jesus' command: "Render to Caesar the things that are Caesar's, and to God the things that are God's"?
2. "Behold, I send you out as sheep in the midst of wolves; so be wise as serpents and innocent as doves." (Matt. 10:16.) What does this commandment of Jesus say about social action?
3. Is evil unchangeable, or can the gospel overcome it? What difference does the answer make in our attitude toward those who practice it?
4. Why is extremism called "idolatry"? How can a dedicated Christian avoid it, while he is witnessing to his faith?

General Questions

1. Does the church have a unique contribution to make in social action? If so, what is it?
2. "Evangelism and social action are opposite sides of the same coin." Do you agree or disagree? Why?
3. Is it possible for dedicated Christians to disagree on social issues? What does this say to "Christian social action"?

Selected Bibliography

[Biclical studies which provide background for chapters 1 and 2.]

Albright, William F., *The Archaeology of Palestine* (Garden City, N. Y.: Doubleday [Penguin series], 1961).

Anderson, Bernhard W., *Understanding the Old Testament* (Englewood Cliffs, N. J.: Prentice Hall, 1957).

Cullmann, Oscar, *Christ and Time; the Primitive Christian Conception of Time and History* (Philadelphia: The Westminster Press, rev. ed., 1964).

Knight, G. A. F., *A Christian Theology of the Old Testament* (Richmond, Va.: John Knox Press, 1959).

Rowley, H. H., ed., *The Old Testament and Modern Study* (New York: Oxford University Press, paperback ed., 1960). A good survey of developments in Old Testament scholarship, 1900-1950.

[Studies of the history of biblical interpretation. Background for chapters 1, 2, and 5.]

Grant, Robert M., "History of the Interpretation of the Bible, I. Ancient Period," in *The Interpreter's Bible*, I, 106 ff. (Nashville: Abingdon Press, 1952).

Greenslade, S. L., *The Cambridge History of the Bible; The West from the Reformation to the Present Day* (New York: Cambridge U. Press, 1963).

Grobel, Kendrick, "Interpretation (of the Bible), History and Principles of," in *The Interpreter's Dictionary of the Bible,* II, 718-24 (Nashville: Abingdon Press, 1962).

Kraeling, Emil, *The Old Testament Since the Reformation* (New York: Harper, 1955). A comprehensive study, in rather technical language.

McNeill, John T., "History of the Interpretation of the Bible, II. Medieval and Reformation Period," *The Interpreter's Bible,* I, 115 ff.

Terrien, Samuel, "History of the Interpretation of the Bible, III. Modern Period," *The Interpreter's Bible,* I, 127 ff.

[Source material and historical summaries which give further background to chapters 4 and 5.]

Furniss, Norman F., *The Fundamentalist Controversy 1918-31* (Hamden, Conn.: Archon Books, 1963). Based on a Ph.D. dissertation at Yale University.

Luccock, Halford; Paul Hutchinson and Robert Goodloe, *The Story of Methodism* (Nashville: Abingdon Press, 1949). A very readable summary of Wesley's life and the growth of Methodism.

Marty, Martin E., *A Short History of Christianity* (Cleveland: The World Publ. Co., Meridian paperback).

Mathews, Shailer, *The Faith of Modernism* (New York: The Macmillan Co., 1924).

Rauschenbusch, Walter, *Christianity and the Social Crisis,* R. D. Cross, ed. (New York: Harper & Row, Torchbook series, paperback).

Rauschenbusch, Walter, *A Theology of the Social Gospel* (Nashville: Abingdon Press, Apex series, paperback).

Schweitzer, Albert, *The Quest for the Historic Jesus* (New York: The Macmillan Co., paperback).

Smith, Timothy, *Revivalism and Social Reform* (Nashville: Abingdon, 1957).

Walker, Williston, *A History of the Christian Church* (New York: Scribner, rev. ed., 1959).

[Further readings on the social upheavals discussed in chapter 5.]

Keynes, J. M., *The End of Laissez-Faire* (London: Hogarth Press, 1927).

Marx, Karl, *Capital* (New York: Modern Library, Inc.). It may seem strange to find a book by Karl Marx listed in a book by a Christian minister for Christian laymen, but all medical school libraries contain books on cancer.

Marx, Karl, *The Communist Manifesto* (New York: Washington Square Press, paperback).

Mills, C. Wright, *The Marxists* (New York: Dell, paperback).

Steffens, Lincoln, *Shame of the Cities* (New York: Hill and Wang, paperback, 1957).

Tawney, R. H., *Religion and the Rise of Capitalism* (New York: The New American Library of World Literature, Inc., Mentor series, paperback).

[Recent summaries of current trends in Protestant theology, for background to chapter 6.]

Hordern, William, *A Layman's Guide to Protestant Theology* (New York: The Macmillan Co., paperback).

Williams, Daniel Day, *What Present Day Theologians Are Thinking* (New York: Harper & Brothers, rev. ed., 1959).

[Recent books dealing with the problems of society from the viewpoint of the Christian faith. Notes and bibliographies in these books will lead the interested reader to other resources.]

Bangs, Carl, *The Communist Encounter* (Kansas City: The Nazarene Publ. Hse., Beacon Hill Press, 1962). Published as a Missions study guide by the Church of the Nazarene.

Berton, Pierre, *The Comfortable Pew* (Philadelphia: Lippincott, 1965).

Bennett, John C., *When Christians Make Political Decisions*. A Reflection Book (New York: Association Press, 1964).

Brademas, John, "Christian Responsibility in the Political Order," *Together* (Dec., 1965), pp. 45-48. An excellent article, written by a layman who is a Member of the U.S. House of Representatives.

Gardiner, Clinton, *Biblical Faith and Social Ethics* (New York: Harper, 1960). A comprehensive survey of the current scene. The best of its kind.

Hordern, William, *Christianity and Communism* (Nashville: Abingdon, paperback, 1962).

140

Obenhaus, Victor, *Ethics for an Industrial Age; a Christian Inquiry* (New York: Harper & Row, 1965). This is the last in a series of books commissioned by the National Council of Churches on "The Ethics and Economics of Society." A list of other books in the series can be obtained from the N.C.C., or from Harper & Row, publishers.

Spike, Robert W., *The Freedom Revolution and The Churches* (New York: Association Press, 1965).

Tilson, C. Everett, *Segregation and the Bible* (Nashville: Abingdon Press, 1958).

Walmsley, Arthur E., *The Church in a Society of Abundance* (New York: Seabury, 1963).

Index

American History, 43-45
Amos, 16, 23-25, 28, 36, 47-49
Ananias, 102-3
Archaeology, 63
Assyria, 24-26, 34, 63

Babylonia, 26-31, 63
Bash, Lawrence, 131
Boston Tea Party, 44

Calvin, John, 52-56
Canaan, land of, 22-23
Chapter Oak incident, 44
Christology, 17, 38-42, 81-83
Church of England, 56
Communism, 89, 121, 129, 130
Conservatism, 86
Creation, doctrine of, 89-90
Cyrus, 30-33

David, King, 22, 35-36
Deism, 53-54

Egypt, 23, 63
Ephesians, letter to the, 87
Esther, book of, 41
Ethiopians, 23
Evangelism, 60-61, 76-78, 103-7, 123
Exile, Babylonian, 26-34
Exodus (event), 16, 45
Extremism, 120-23

Ezra, 12, 21, 32-37

Fundamentalism, 74-76, 83-87

Genesis, 21, 29
Goldwater, Barry, 19
Grace, doctrine of, 87-89, 93-98

Habakkuk, 30-31
Hegel, 66, 84
Historicism, 62
Holy Spirit, 38
Hosea, book of, 15, 45
Hutton, James, 64

Idolatry, 13, 24, 48-49, 120-21
Incarnation, doctrine of, 69, 81, 86-89, 93-95, 100
Institutionalism, 56
Integration, 20-21, 45
Isaiah, 15, 16, 23-24, 50, 115

James II, of England, 44
Jeremiah, 24, 115
Jerusalem, 13, 22, 24, 27, 31
John, first letter of, 98-99
John, Gospel of, 69, 98
John Birch Society, 109
Johnson, Lyndon, 19
Jonah, 34-36
Joshua, book of, 15
Judaism, 14-16, 101

Judges, book of, 12, 15

King James Version, 91, 131
Kingdom of God, 69-70

Laissez faire, 54
Leviticus, 13, 16
Liberalism, Protestant, 70-73, 79-86
Lincoln, Abraham, 44
Love, doctrine of, 93-106
Luther, Martin, 52

Marx, Karl, 88
Mesopotamia, 24, 26
Methodist Church, 58-61, 75-77
Modernism, Protestant, 70-74
Mordecai, 12, 41
Moses, 42, 46

Nationalism, Jewish, 32, 36
Nebuchadnezzar, 26
Nehemiah, 21, 32-35
New English Bible, 91
Numbers, book of, 45

Oral tradition, 27, 64, 129
Orthodoxy, Protestant, 54-57, 76-78, 92

Passover, 16
Paul, 46, 68, 85, 89, 95, 101-3
Persia, 30-33
Peter, Simon, 100
Philistines, 22-23, 126
Picketing, 115
Pornography, 109
Predestination, 54-56, 127
Presbyterian Church, 54-55
Priesthood, Jewish, 27-30
Psalms, book of, 13

Rationalism, 53-54
Rauschenbusch, Walter, 72, 79
Reaction, 86

Reformation, Protestant, 46, 52-56
Revelation, book of, 11
Revelation, doctrine of, 90-92
Revised Standard Version, 91, 131
Romans, Paul's letter to the, 55
Ruth, 35-36

Samaritans, 25
Samuel, books of, 80
Schweitzer, Albert, 82-83
Science, 64-69, 73-74
Second Isaiah, 31-33, 126
Segregation, 20-21
Septuagint, 11, 125
Sermon on the Mount, 69
Sin, doctrine of, 87-89, 95-97
Slavery, 60
Smith, Timothy, 130
Social gospel, 70-73, 97-101
Socialism, 72-73
Suburbia, 48-49
Suffering Servant, 15, 31-33
Syria, 23

Temple, Jerusalem, 27-30, 33, 109
Thomas, Norman, 73, 130
Together magazine, 112
Tower, Senator John, 112
Trinity, doctrine of, 38-39
Typology, 42-43

United Nations, 109
Universalism, Jewish, 34, 36

Walker, Alan, 77
War on Poverty, 109
Wesley, John, 46, 57-61
Whitefield, George, 58
World War I, 82, 85
World War II, 85

Xerxes I, 33